the Any Oven Cookbook

MICROWAVE/CONVENTIONAL RECIPES from Saran Wrap ™

A Benjamin Company Book

Cover photo: Bran Muffins (page 127), Strawberry Rhubarb
Soufflé (page 143), Spring Vegetables (page 82),
Fruit Stuffed Pork Loin (page 52) with Apricot
Sauce (page 104), Plum Conserve (page 111)

Recipe Development:	Martha Reynolds
Editor:	Barbara Bloch
Production:	Beth Kukkonen
Art Director:	Tom Brecklin
Color Photography:	Walter Storck
Typography:	A-Line, Milwaukee

Copyright © 1981 The Dow Chemical Company
All rights reserved.

Prepared and produced by The Benjamin Company, Inc.
485 Madison Avenue
New York, New York 10022

ISBN: 0-87502-083-6
Library of Congress Card Catalog Number: 80-66315

Printed in the United States of America
First Printing: January, 1981

SARAN WRAP™ brand plastic film is a trademark of
The Dow Chemical Company, Indianapolis, Indiana.

CONTENTS

Introduction

Are there holes in your microwave story?

Just about everyone who has experienced the pleasure of microwave cooking knows how easy it is to pop a chicken leg, frozen casserole, leftovers or other food into a microwave oven for quick, delicious cooking. It is a freezer-to-oven story that demonstrates the time-saving advances of the twentieth century — a happy marriage of convenience and economy.

But cooks who mistakenly believe that all plastic wraps work equally well in either freezer or microwave oven, and therefore use whatever wrap they happen to have on hand, are likely to find holes in both their point of view and their plastic wrap. There is only one wrap that seals in moisture in the freezer and withstands high temperatures in a microwave oven with consistently superior results. Other wraps do not provide as much protection against freezer burn as SARAN WRAP™ brand plastic film and, in addition, other wraps often melt, develop holes or cause other serious problems when used in a microwave oven. Eventually most cooks discover through sad experience that all plastic wraps are not created equal.

The use of SARAN WRAP has provided consumers with superior food storage protection in the refrigerator and the freezer for over 25 years. It is proving just as effective in microwave cooking. Although many other plastic films have been available over the years, none have been able to provide equally high quality protection. Why? Because SARAN WRAP is made from an entirely different plastic produced by a different manufacturing process from other plastic wraps and therefore offers qualities other wraps cannot match.

SARAN WRAP is made from saran plastic resin manufactured by The Dow Chemical Company under the chemical name of polyvinylidene chloride (PVDC). It is this plastic resin that gives SARAN WRAP its high-temperature tolerance as well as resistance to solvents such as hot fats and oils. This unique resin provides the superior barrier that keeps moisture in and undesirable tastes and odors out of food wrapped in SARAN WRAP.

The other plastic wraps purchased today are made of resins that have a different chemical composition from the resin used in SARAN WRAP. Polyvinyl chloride (PVC) films, used by most grocery retailers, and the polyethylene (PE) films do not form as effective a barrier as SARAN WRAP. And because they have a lower melting temperature than SARAN WRAP they are vulnerable to hot fats and oils.

SARAN WRAP has been shown to preserve the quality of food better and longer in the freezer than other films because it provides a superior barrier to moisture and gases. Moreover, it helps assure fast and uniform cooking and improves the flavor and appearance of food cooked in a microwave oven.

Temperature Characteristics

The plastic resin in PVDC provides SARAN WRAP with greater resistance to destruction from high temperature and solvents than any other plastic wrap. The softening temperature of SARAN WRAP is 250°F (120°C) compared with 195°F (90°C) for PE and 200°F (about 95°C) for PVC. Since food cooked in a microwave oven often reaches temperatures above boiling, 212°F (100°C) a high softening temperature for plastic wrap used in a microwave oven is crucial for satisfactory performance. SARAN WRAP resists the melting that makes it so difficult to remove other plastic wraps from cooked food. In addition, SARAN WRAP does not rupture or form large holes during microwave cooking the way other wraps do. SARAN WRAP will not dissolve when it comes into contact with the hot fats and oils that often act as solvents in microwave cooking and cause problems with other plastic wrap.

Advantages in Microwave Cooking

There are many advantages to using SARAN WRAP in microwave cooking. Since microwaves cook from the outer edge of the food toward the center, uneven cooking often occurs. Research shows that when a dish is covered with SARAN WRAP, steam that normally escapes from around the edges of the dish is retained and as a result minimizes uneven cooking. In addition to improving heat distribution the use of SARAN WRAP also improves the texture, taste and appearance of microcooked food.

A SARAN WRAP cover also helps to reduce and even eliminate oven spattering and it will help keep juices in the food where they belong rather than on the surface of the oven where they must be cleaned up.

The use of SARAN WRAP in microwave cooking is not limited to covering for bowls or dishes. It can be turned into a container as well. Appropriate foods can be wrapped in SARAN WRAP, properly vented and cooked right in the wrap. They will cook evenly and you will have fewer dishes to wash. It is even possible to wrap food in SARAN WRAP, freeze it, thaw it and cook it without ever using a dish.

It is important to remember that when SARAN WRAP is used as a cover or a container in a microwave oven it must be vented to allow excess steam to escape. Instead of tucking SARAN WRAP firmly around a container, leave one edge loose and turn it back slightly to provide a vent. Leave a seam along the top of the food wrapped in SARAN WRAP so steam can escape without allowing juices to run out. Holes should not be poked into SARAN WRAP as this can cause tearing. Use caution when you unwrap food, making sure the vent or seam faces away from you so you will not be burned by hot steam.

For further information, write to:

Nan Collinson, Manager
Consumer Communications
The Dow Chemical Company
P.O. Box 68511
Indianapolis, Indiana 46268

Note: Do not use SARAN WRAP with a browning unit and, of course, remember it cannot be used in either a conventional or convection oven.

Appetizing Appetizers

SHERRIED CRAB DIP

Microwave Cooking Time: 5 minutes
Conventional Cooking Time: 20 minutes

10 servings

1 package (8 ounces) cream cheese, softened
3 tablespoons medium-dry sherry
1 teaspoon Worcestershire sauce
1 teaspoon lemon juice
1/8 teaspoon hot pepper sauce
Salt to taste
1 can (6 1/2 ounces) crabmeat, drained
1/4 cup sliced almonds, toasted
Crackers

Microwave: Stir cream cheese in 3-cup glass bowl or microsafe serving dish until smooth. Add sherry, Worcestershire sauce, lemon juice, hot pepper sauce and salt. Stir well. Pick over crabmeat, discarding any pieces of cartilage and shell. Stir into cream cheese mixture. Cover tightly with SARAN WRAP, turning back edge to vent. Microcook at 50% power 5 minutes until hot and bubbly. Stir 3 times while cooking. Season to taste with salt. Sprinkle with almonds, let stand 3 minutes then serve with crackers.

Conventional: Preheat oven to 350°. Prepare cream cheese and crab mixture as directed in microwave method. Spoon mixture into small baking dish and bake 15 to 20 minutes, or until hot and bubbly. Sprinkle with almonds and serve with crackers.

Nice to know: You can soften cream cheese in microwave oven. Unwrap cheese and place on plate. Microcook at 30% power 2 to 2 1/2 minutes or until soft, turning cheese over once.

DEVILED MUSHROOMS

Microwave Cooking Time: 3 minutes   *12 appetizers*
Conventional Cooking Time: 12 minutes

12 medium-size mushrooms
     (about 1 1/2 inches
     in diameter)
   Salt
1/2 cup minced ham
  2 tablespoons finely
     chopped shallots

1 tablespoon prepared
   mustard
2 teaspoons mayonnaise
   Dash pepper
3 or 4 pimiento-stuffed
   green olives, sliced

Microwave: Wipe mushrooms gently with damp cloth. Remove stems carefully and reserve for another purpose. Place mushroom caps, rounded-side down, around the edge of large microsafe dinner plate. Sprinkle very lightly with salt. Mix ham, shallots, mustard, mayonnaise and pepper. Spoon into mushroom caps. Top with olive slices. Microcook at 100% power 3 minutes, rotating plate once. Let stand 2 minutes. Arrange on platter and serve immediately.

Conventional: Preheat oven to 375°. Prepare mushrooms and ham mixture as directed in microwave method. Spoon ham mixture into mushrooms and place in 8-inch baking dish. Bake 12 minutes. Top with olive slices, arrange on platter and serve immediately.

TUNA MOUSSE

Microwave Cooking Time: 4 minutes   *4 to 6 servings*
Conventional Cooking Time: 40 minutes

2 cans (7 ounces each)
   tuna, drained
1 small onion, quartered
2 tablespoons lemon juice
1/4 teaspoon dill

   Dash pepper
1/4 cup mayonnaise
  2 egg whites
  2 tablespoons chopped
     parsley

Microwave: Grease 1-quart fluted glass mold or bowl. Place tuna, onion, lemon juice, dill and pepper in food processor or blender. Process until finely chopped. Place in mixing bowl and stir in mayonnaise. Beat egg whites until soft peaks form. Fold in tuna mixture with parsley. Spoon into prepared mold. Cover tightly with SARAN WRAP, turning back edge to vent. Microcook at 70% power 1 minute. Stir cooked edges to center. Recover, leaving vent, and microcook 3 minutes longer, stirring after

1 1/2 minutes. Let stand, covered, 5 minutes. Cover mold with serving dish and turn upside down to unmold. Serve warm or chilled.

Conventional: Preheat oven to 375°. Prepare tuna mixture and spoon into mold as directed in microwave method. Set mold on rack in large pan and place in oven. Add enough boiling water to pan to come halfway up side of mold. Bake 40 to 50 minutes or until knife inserted in center comes out clean. Cover mold with serving dish and turn upside down to unmold. Serve warm or chilled.

MEXICO CHILI-CHEESE APPETIZER

Microwave Cooking Time: 12 1/2 minutes   *10 servings*
Conventional Cooking Time: 35 minutes

1/4 cup butter or margarine	1 cup creamy cottage
1/4 cup yellow cornmeal	cheese
1 teaspoon baking powder	1 can (4 ounces) chopped
1/2 teaspoon salt	green chilies
4 eggs, beaten	
1 cup chopped or shredded Muenster cheese	

Microwave: Grease 8-inch round glass cake dish. Place butter in glass mixing bowl. Cover tightly with SARAN WRAP, turning back edge to vent. Microcook at 100% power 1 1/2 minutes. Stir in cornmeal, baking powder and salt and mix until smooth. Stir in eggs, cheese and chilies. Recover, leaving vent, and microcook at 50% power 8 minutes, stirring every 2 minutes until mixture is hot and cheese is melted. Pour into prepared cake dish. Cover tightly with SARAN WRAP, turning back edge to vent. Microcook at 100% power 3 to 4 minutes or until knife inserted about 1 inch from center comes out clean. Let stand, covered, on heatproof surface, 5 minutes. Cut into wedges.

Conventional: Grease 8-inch square or round baking dish. Preheat oven to 325°. Melt butter in medium-size saucepan. Add remaining ingredients, stirring until smooth. Pour into prepared baking dish. Bake 30 to 35 minutes or until knife inserted in center comes out clean. Cut into wedges.

Menu hint: This appetizer also makes a delightful luncheon dish for 4 to 6 people. Serve with Mexican Pepper Salad (page 96), crisp taco chips and fresh fruit for dessert.

SHRIMP AND CHEESE CANAPES

Microwave Cooking Time: 5 minutes   *20 appetizers*
Conventional Cooking Time: 13 minutes

1/4 **pound cleaned, frozen shrimp**	1 **teaspoon lemon juice**
1 **cup shredded Swiss cheese**	1/4 **teaspoon salt**
	1/8 **teaspoon thyme**
1/2 **cup fresh bread crumbs (1 slice)**	20 **slices party rye bread or crisp crackers**
1/3 **cup mayonnaise**	**Fresh dill for garnish**

Microwave: Place 1/2 cup water in 2-cup glass measure. Cover tightly with SARAN WRAP, turning back edge to vent. Microcook at 100% power 2 minutes or until boiling. Add frozen shrimp. Recover, leaving vent, and microcook at 100% power 1 1/2 minutes or until shrimp turn pink. Let stand 3 minutes.

Drain shrimp well and chop. Mix chopped shrimp, cheese, bread crumbs, mayonnaise, lemon juice, salt and thyme. Spoon small mounds of shrimp mixture on each piece of bread. Arrange 10 canapes on 12-inch round microsafe platter. Microcook at 90% power 1 to 1 1/2 minutes or until shrimp mixture is hot, rotating once. Repeat with remaining canapes. Garnish with tiny pieces of dill and serve immediately.

Conventional: Heat 1 cup water to boiling. Add shrimp, cover and cook 3 minutes or until shrimp turn pink. Prepare shrimp mixture and spoon onto bread as directed in microwave method. Preheat broiler. Place canapes on rack of broiler pan. Broil 9 to 10 minutes or until tops are lightly browned and mixture is hot. Garnish with tiny pieces of dill and serve immediately.

Nice to know: On a busy day you can make the shrimp mixture early, cover with SARAN WRAP and refrigerate. Assemble and microcook or broil just before serving.

Wrapped Chicken Livers (page 12),
Marinated Chicken Wings (page 12),
Shrimp and Cheese Canapés

WRAPPED CHICKEN LIVERS

Microwave Cooking Time: 8 minutes   *20 appetizers*
Conventional Cooking Time: 12 minutes

1/2 cup medium-dry sherry	1/2 teaspoon salt
1 1/2 teaspoons dry mustard	10 chicken livers (about
1/4 teaspoon hot pepper	3/4 pound)
sauce	10 slices bacon, halved

Microwave: Prepare marinade by mixing sherry, mustard, hot pepper sauce and salt. Cut each chicken liver in half and add to marinade. Cover tightly with SARAN WRAP and refrigerate 2 to 3 hours, stirring occasionally. Place bacon on double layer of paper towels. Cover with paper towel and microcook at 100% power 2 minutes. Remove chicken livers from marinade with slotted spoon. Wrap piece of bacon around each liver half. Secure with wooden toothpicks. Arrange 10 appetizers around edge of microsafe plate. Microcook at 100% power 3 minutes. Repeat with remaining 10 appetizers. Serve immediately.

Conventional: Cut and marinate chicken livers as directed in microwave method. Preheat broiler. Remove chicken livers from marinade with slotted spoon. Wrap piece of raw bacon around each liver half. Secure with wooden toothpicks. Place on broiler pan. Broil 10 to 12 minutes or until bacon is browned, turning once. Serve immediately.

MARINATED CHICKEN WINGS

Microwave Cooking Time: 19 minutes   *24 appetizers*
Conventional Cooking Time: 34 minutes

1/4 cup Dijon-style mustard	1 clove garlic, minced
3 tablespoons honey	12 chicken wings
2 tablespoons dry white	2 cups herb-seasoned
wine	stuffing mix, crushed
1/2 teaspoon salt	
1/4 teaspoon browning sauce	
(optional)	

Microwave: Combine mustard, honey, wine, salt, browning sauce and garlic in 1 1/2-quart glass bowl or casserole. Cut each chicken wing into 3 pieces at the joints. Save wing tips to make stock another time. Add wing sections to mustard marinade. Stir well to coat. Cover tightly with SARAN WRAP and refrigerate at least 2 hours or overnight. Remove chicken wings from marinade and dip into stuffing mix to coat. Reserve marinade. Arrange 12 wing sections around edge of 12-inch microsafe plate. Microcook at 100% power 8 minutes, rotating plate once. Repeat with remaining sections. Add 2 tablespoons water to marinade. Cover tightly with SARAN WRAP, turning back edge to vent. Microcook at 100% power 3 minutes or until boiling. Serve as dipping sauce with chicken wings.

Conventional: Prepare and store mustard marinade and cut chicken wings as directed in microwave method. Preheat oven to 375°. Remove chicken wings from marinade and dip into stuffing mix to coat. Reserve marinade. Place chicken wings on large cookie sheet. Bake 25 to 30 minutes or until browned and crisp. Add 2 tablespoons water to marinade. Stir until smooth. Pour into small saucepan and heat to boiling. Reduce heat and simmer 2 minutes. Serve as dipping sauce with chicken wings.

CHILI CON QUESO

Microwave Cooking Time: 11 minutes   *12 servings*
Conventional Cooking Time: 17 minutes

1 small onion, minced	1 can (4 ounces) chopped
1 clove garlic, minced	green chilies
2 tablespoons butter or	1/2 pound Monterey Jack
margarine	cheese, shredded
2 medium-size tomatoes,	Taco chips for dipping
peeled and diced	

Microwave: Combine onion, garlic and butter in 3-cup ceramic saucepan. Cover tightly with SARAN WRAP, turning back edge to vent. Microcook at 100% power 3 minutes, stirring once. Add tomatoes and green chilies. Stir to combine. Recover, leaving vent, and microcook at 100% power 6 minutes, stirring once. Add cheese and stir well. Recover and microcook at 50% power 2 minutes or until cheese melts and mixture is hot. Stir well and serve immediately with taco chips.

Conventional: Sauté onion and garlic in butter until onion is transparent, about 5 minutes. Add tomatoes and green chilies. Heat to simmering, stirring constantly. Cover and simmer 10 minutes, stirring frequently. (Add 1 tablespoon water if mixture becomes dry.) Add cheese and cook, stirring, until cheese melts and is smooth, about 2 minutes. Serve immediately with taco chips.

TEXAS TACO DIP

Microwave Cooking Time: 15 minutes   *20 servings*
Conventional Cooking Time: 23 minutes

1/2 pound lean ground beef	1 tablespoon chili powder
1 onion, chopped	3/4 teaspoon salt
1 clove garlic, minced	1 cup shredded sharp
1 can (15 ounces) red	Cheddar cheese, divided
kidney beans, mashed	1/2 cup chopped pimiento-
with liquid	stuffed green olives
1/2 cup tomato sauce	Taco chips

Microwave: Combine meat, onion and garlic in 1 1/2-quart glass bowl or casserole. Stir to break up meat. Cover tightly with SARAN WRAP, turning back edge to vent. Microcook at 100% power 4 minutes, stirring twice. Drain off excess fat. Add beans, tomato sauce, chili powder and salt. Mix well. Recover, leaving vent, and microcook at 100% power 3 minutes. Stir well, recover and microcook at 50% power 8 minutes, stirring once. Stir in 1/2 cup cheese. Spoon into chafing dish and set over low flame or simmering water. Sprinkle with remaining 1/2 cup cheese and olives. Serve with taco chips.

Conventional: Sauté meat, onion and garlic in skillet until onion is transparent and meat is lightly browned. Drain off excess fat. Stir in mashed beans, tomato sauce, chili powder and salt. Heat to boiling, stirring constantly. Reduce heat, cover and simmer 15 minutes. Stir in 1/2 cup cheese. Serve as directed in microwave method.

CHICKEN LIVER PATE

Microwave Cooking Time: 10 minutes   *2 cups*
Conventional Cooking Time: 15 minutes

2 onions, chopped	1/4 cup dry sherry (use
1/4 cup butter or margarine	1/3 cup in
1 pound chicken livers	conventional method)
2 teaspoons prepared	Dash hot pepper sauce
mustard	Lettuce leaves
3/4 teaspoon salt	Crackers or rye bread

Microwave: Lightly grease 2- to 2 1/2-cup mold. Combine onions and butter in 1 1/2-quart glass bowl or casserole. Cover tightly with SARAN WRAP, turning back edge to vent. Microcook at 100% power 2 minutes. Add chicken livers, mustard and salt.

Recover, leaving vent, and microcook at 70% power 5 minutes, stirring once. Add sherry and hot pepper sauce. Recover and microcook at 100% power 3 minutes. Cool to room temperature. Spoon into blender or food processor and process until smooth. Pour into prepared mold and chill until firm. Unmold onto plate, surround with lettuce and serve with crackers.

Conventional: Lightly grease 2- to 2 1/2-cup mold. Sauté onions in butter until transparent, about 3 minutes. Add livers and sauté until lightly browned, about 5 minutes. Stir in mustard, salt, 1/3 cup sherry and hot pepper sauce. Heat to boiling. Reduce heat, cover and simmer 7 minutes. Cool to room temperature. Process, mold, and serve pâté according to directions in microwave method.

SWEDISH MEATBALLS

Microwave Cooking Time: 15 minutes   *40 meatballs*
Conventional Cooking Time: 30 minutes

1 pound lean ground beef	1 cup beef broth
1 cup dry bread crumbs	2 tablespoons all-purpose
1 onion, minced	flour (use 1/4 cup in
1/3 cup dry sherry	conventional
3/4 cup half-and-half,	method)
divided	Chopped parsley for
3/4 teaspoon salt	garnish
1/4 teaspoon nutmeg	1/4 cup butter or margarine
1/4 teaspoon thyme	(in conventional
1/4 teaspoon oregano	method only)

Microwave: Mix beef, bread crumbs, onion, sherry, 1/4 cup half-and-half, salt, nutmeg, thyme and oregano until well-blended. Shape into 40 1-inch meatballs. Place in 1-quart casserole. Cover tightly with SARAN WRAP, turning back edge to vent. Microcook at 100% power 5 minutes, stirring once. Drain. Mix remaining 1/2 cup half-and-half, beef broth and flour until smooth. Pour over meatballs. Recover, leaving vent, and microcook at 70% power 10 minutes, stirring once. Serve with toothpicks or on small plates to be eaten with fork.

Conventional: Mix and shape meatballs as directed in microwave method. Coat with 1/4 cup flour. Heat 1/4 cup butter in skillet. Add meatballs and sauté until lightly browned. Add remaining 1/2 cup half-and-half and beef broth. Heat to simmering, cover and simmer 20 minutes. Serve as above.

EGGPLANT CAVIAR

Microwave Cooking Time: 33 minutes　　　　　　　　　*30 servings*
Conventional Cooking Time: 65 minutes

1 onion, finely chopped	1/4 cup chopped pimiento-stuffed green olives or salad olives
1 green pepper, finely chopped	
2 cloves garlic, minced	2 teaspoons sugar
1/4 cup olive oil	1 teaspoon basil
1 eggplant (about 1 pound), peeled and diced	1/4 teaspoon pepper
1 can (6 ounces) tomato paste	1/2 teaspoon salt
1/4 cup red wine vinegar	Cocktail rye, pumpernickel or crisp crackers

Microwave:　Combine onion, green pepper, garlic and oil in 2-quart casserole. Cover tightly with SARAN WRAP, turning back edge to vent. Microcook at 100% power 5 minutes. Stir in eggplant, tomato paste, vinegar, olives, sugar, basil, pepper and salt. Recover, leaving vent, and microcook at 100% power 10 minutes, stirring once. Stir well, recover, and microcook at 70% power 18 minutes, stirring once. Chill and serve with small slices of bread or crackers.

Conventional:　Sauté onion, green pepper and garlic in oil in skillet until onion is transparent. Add eggplant, tomato paste, vinegar, olives, sugar, basil, pepper and salt. Cover and simmer 1 hour, stirring occasionally. Chill and serve with small slices of bread or crackers.

CHINESE-STYLE RIBS

Microwave Cooking Time: 35 minutes　　　*Approximately 15 appetizers*
Conventional Cooking Time: 90 minutes

1/3 cup soy sauce	1 teaspoon ginger
1/3 cup dark corn syrup	1 teaspoon prepared horseradish
2 tablespoons dry sherry	
2 tablespoons thick steak sauce	2 pounds pork spare ribs, cut into 1-rib sections

Microwave:　Mix soy sauce, corn syrup, sherry, steak sauce, ginger and horseradish. Place ribs in bowl and add sauce. Cover tightly with SARAN WRAP and refrigerate at least 2 hours, stirring occasionally. Remove ribs from bowl and reserve sauce.

Place ribs on rack in shallow 10-inch square casserole. Cover with SARAN WRAP, turning back edge to vent. Microcook at 70% power 20 minutes, stirring ribs once. Uncover and brush with sauce. Microcook at 70% power 15 minutes until glazed and tender, brushing with sauce 2 or 3 times.

Conventional: Mix sauce and marinate ribs as directed in microwave method. Preheat oven to 350°. Remove ribs from sauce and place in shallow baking pan. Bake 1 1/2 hours or until glazed and tender, brushing occasionally with sauce.

SWISS APPETIZER FONDUE

Microwave Cooking Time: 5 1/2 minutes   *6 servings*
Conventional Cooking Time: 8 minutes

1 clove garlic, halved	2 cups shredded Swiss
3/4 cup dry white wine	cheese (1/2 pound)
1 tablespoon cornstarch	1 medium-size loaf French
(use 2 teaspoons in	bread, cut into chunks
conventional method)	and heated
Dash nutmeg	2 apples, cored and cut
Dash freshly ground	into chunks
pepper	
1 tablespoon applejack,	
brandy, kirsch or	
lemon juice	

Microwave: Rub inside of 1-quart casserole or microsafe serving dish with cut surface of garlic. Discard garlic. Combine wine, cornstarch, nutmeg and pepper in dish and stir until smooth. Cover tightly with SARAN WRAP, turning back edge to vent. Microcook at 100% power 2 1/2 minutes, stirring twice. Stir in applejack. Gradually add cheese, stirring until mixture is smooth. Recover, leaving vent, and microcook at 50% power 3 minutes or until steaming hot, stirring twice. Spoon into chafing dish and keep warm over low flame or simmering water. Use fondue forks to spear bread and apple pieces and dip them into fondue.

Conventional: Using fondue pot, prepare mixture as directed in microwave method. Heat slowly to simmering and cook 1 minute. Stir in applejack. Gradually add cheese, stirring until mixture is smooth. Heat over very low heat about 5 minutes. Serve in fondue pot and as directed in microwave method.

CHICKEN PINEAPPLE KABOBS

Microwave Cooking Time: 8 minutes   *16 appetizers*
Conventional Cooking Time: 10 minutes

1 can (15 1/4 ounces) pineapple chunks	1 clove garlic, halved
1/4 cup cider vinegar	2 chicken cutlets (about
2 tablespoons soy sauce	1/2 pound each)
1/2 teaspoon ginger	1 large green pepper, cut
1/2 teaspoon salt	into 16 squares

Microwave: Drain and reserve juice from pineapple. Set pineapple chunks aside. Add vinegar, soy sauce, ginger, salt and garlic to juice. Cut chicken breasts into 3/4-inch cubes (about 48 pieces). Add to marinade. Cover tightly with SARAN WRAP and refrigerate 3 hours, stirring occasionally. Alternately skewer 3 pieces of chicken and 2 pieces of pineapple on sixteen 10-inch wooden skewers. Lay 8 filled skewers across a 12 × 8-inch glass baking dish. Microcook at 100% power 2 minutes. Add 1 piece green pepper to each skewer. Move center skewers to outside edge of dish and outside skewers to center of dish. Microcook at 100% power 2 minutes longer. Repeat with remaining 8 skewers. Serve immediately.

Conventional: Drain juice from pineapple. Prepare marinade, cut chicken and assemble as directed in microwave method, using metal skewers. Preheat broiler. Place skewers on rack in broiler pan. Broil 10 to 12 minutes or until chicken is fork-tender, turning skewers over once. Add 1 piece green pepper to each skewer when turning for last 5 or 6 minutes of broiling. Serve immediately.

Nice to know: If you want to use wooden skewers in conventional method, be sure to soak skewers in water at least 1 hour to prevent them from catching fire during broiling.

DOLMATHES

Microwave Cooking Time: 37 minutes　　　　　　　　*30 appetizers*
Conventional Cooking Time: 50 minutes

2 onions, minced	2 teaspoons grated lemon peel
2 cloves garlic, minced	
3 tablespoons olive oil	3/4 teaspoon salt
3/4 cup long grain rice	About 30 pickled grape leaves, rinsed
1/2 cup lemon juice, divided	
	Parsley or dill stems (optional)
1 tablespoon dry dill or 3 tablespoons chopped fresh dill	Plain yogurt
	Lemon wedges

Microwave: Combine onions, garlic and olive oil in 1-quart casserole. Cover tightly with SARAN WRAP, turning back edge to vent. Microcook at 100% power 5 minutes, stirring once. Add 1 1/4 cups water, rice, 1/4 cup lemon juice, dill, lemon peel and salt. Recover, leaving vent, and microcook at 70% power 12 minutes. Cool slightly.

Place grape leaves on cutting surface, shiny side down, and trim off tough stems. Place 1 tablespoon rice mixture on stem end of each leaf. Fold sides over and roll toward tip. Place, tip edge down, in 2-quart casserole, making 2 or 3 layers. Sprinkle parsley stems between layers. Pour 1 cup water and remaining 1/4 cup lemon juice over leaves. Top with a small microsafe plate. Set 1-cup glass measure, right side up, on plate. Cover with SARAN WRAP, pulling it tightly over measuring cup so plate is pushed firmly against grape leaves. (Do not vent.) Microcook at 100% power 5 minutes. Rotate dish and microcook at 50% power 15 minutes longer. Cool with plate and measuring cup in place. Serve at room temperature or well chilled with yogurt and lemon wedges.

Conventional: Sauté onion and garlic in olive oil until onion is transparent. Stir in 1 1/2 cups water, rice, 1/4 cup lemon juice, dill, lemon peel and salt. Simmer 10 minutes. Cool slightly. Fill grape leaves as above and place in 10-inch skillet. Sprinkle parsley stems between layers. Add 1 cup water and remaining 1/4 cup lemon juice. Place plate on top of leaves and weigh down with heavy can or pie plate partially filled with water. Simmer gently 35 minutes, adding more water to skillet if necessary. Cool with weight in place. Serve at room temperature or well chilled with yogurt and lemon wedges.

Nice to know: Stuffed grape leaves are a traditional Middle-Eastern dish, usually served as an accompaniment to a main dish.

Savory Soups

FRESH TOMATO SOUP

Microwave Cooking Time: 23 minutes
Conventional Cooking Time: 35 minutes

4 servings

- 1 onion, finely chopped
- 1/4 cup butter or margarine
- 2 tablespoons olive oil
- 2 pounds ripe tomatoes, cored and coarsely diced
- 1 can (10 3/4 ounces) condensed chicken broth, undiluted
- 2 tablespoons chopped fresh basil or 1 teaspoon dry basil
- 2 teaspoons chopped fresh thyme or 1/2 teaspoon dry thyme
- 2 teaspoons sugar
- 2 tablespoons cornstarch
- 1/2 cup half-and-half or heavy cream (optional)
- Salt and freshly ground pepper to taste

Microwave: Combine onion, butter and oil in 3-quart glass bowl. Cover tightly with SARAN WRAP, turning back edge to vent. Microcook at 100% power 3 minutes. Stir in tomatoes, chicken broth, 1 soup can of water, basil, thyme and sugar. Recover, leaving vent, and microcook at 100% power 17 minutes, stirring once. Press through fine sieve. Discard seeds and skin. Mix cornstarch and 3 tablespoons water until smooth. Stir into soup. Microcook at 100% power 3 to 4 minutes or until mixture boils. Stir in half-and-half, season with salt and pepper and serve.

Conventional: Sauté onion in butter and oil until onion is transparent. Add tomatoes, chicken broth, basil, thyme and sugar. Heat to boiling. Reduce heat, cover, and simmer 30 minutes. Press soup through fine sieve. Discard seeds and skin. Mix cornstarch and 3 tablespoons water until smooth. Stir into soup. Heat to boiling. Boil 1 minute. Stir in half-and-half, season with salt and pepper and serve.

LENTIL SOUP

Microwave Cooking Time: 48 minutes   *6 servings*
Conventional Cooking Time: 55 minutes

6 slices bacon, diced
2 onions, chopped
1 stalk celery, chopped
3 carrots, chopped
1 pound lentils, rinsed
2 cans (10 1/2 ounces each)
    condensed beef broth,
    undiluted

1 bay leaf
Salt and pepper to
    taste
Sieved hard-cooked egg
    for garnish

Microwave: Combine bacon, onions, celery and carrots in 4-quart casserole. Cover tightly with SARAN WRAP, turning back edge to vent. Microcook at 100% power 8 minutes, stirring once. Add lentils, beef broth, bay leaf, salt, pepper and 3 cups hot tap water. Recover, leaving vent, and microcook at 100% power 10 minutes. Stir well, recover and microcook at 70% power 30 minutes or until lentils are tender, stirring once or twice. Let stand 5 minutes. Remove bay leaf and serve garnished with sieved hard-cooked egg.

Conventional: Sauté bacon, onions and celery in large saucepan until onions are transparent and bacon is crisp. Stir in carrots, lentils, beef broth, bay leaf, salt, pepper and 4 cups water. Heat to boiling. Reduce heat, cover and simmer 40 minutes or until lentils are tender. Serve as above.

CREAM OF SPINACH SOUP

Microwave Cooking Time: 13 1/2 minutes   *4 servings*
Conventional Cooking Time: 15 minutes

2 packages (10 ounces
    each) fresh spinach
1 onion, chopped
2 tablespoons butter or
    margarine
1/2 teaspoon salt

Dash pepper
Dash nutmeg
2 cups half-and-half
Dash hot pepper sauce
Watercress for garnish

Microwave: Rinse spinach in several changes of water. Remove stems and discard. Drain. Combine onion and butter in 3-quart casserole. Cover tightly with SARAN WRAP, turning back edge to vent. Microcook at 100% power 3 minutes. Stir in salt, pepper and nutmeg. Add spinach, recover, leaving vent, and microcook at 100% power 4 1/2 minutes or until spinach is wilted and tender. Transfer to food processor or blender and process until finely chopped. Return to casserole, add half-and-half and mix well. Recover, leaving vent, and microcook at 70% power 6 minutes, stirring twice. Spoon into small soup cups and garnish with watercress.

Conventional: Prepare spinach as directed in microwave method. Sauté onion and butter in saucepan until onion is transparent. Stir in seasonings. Add spinach, cover and cook just until spinach wilts, 4 to 5 minutes. Blend as above. Return to saucepan, add half-and-half and mix well. Heat gently until just hot. Serve as above.

Nice to know: *If you prefer, use 1 package (10 ounces) frozen spinach instead of fresh spinach. Either way, this is an elegant soup.*

PEANUT SOUP

Microwave Cooking Time: 12 minutes   *6 servings*
Conventional Cooking Time: 15 minutes

1 medium-size onion, minced	Dash cayenne
	Dash thyme
3 tablespoons butter or margarine	2 1/2 cups chicken broth
	1/3 cup creamy peanut butter
2 tablespoons all-purpose flour	1/2 cup half-and-half or heavy cream
1/4 teaspoon salt or to taste	Sliced scallions for garnish

Microwave: Combine onion and butter in 2 1/2-quart glass bowl. Cover tightly with SARAN WRAP, turning back edge to vent. Microcook at 100% power 4 minutes. Blend in flour, salt, cayenne and thyme until smooth. Gradually stir in chicken broth, then peanut butter. Recover, leaving vent, and microcook at 100% power 8 minutes, stirring twice. Stir in half-and-half. Let stand, covered, 5 minutes. Ladle into small bowls and sprinkle with scallions.

Conventional: Sauté onion in butter until onion is transparent. Blend in flour, salt, cayenne and thyme until smooth. Add chicken broth, stirring to prevent lumping. Add peanut butter. Heat to just boiling, stirring constantly. Reduce heat, cover and simmer 5 minutes. Add half-and-half, simmer until just heated. Serve as above.

Nice to know: *If you are watching calories, substitute skim milk for cream.*

CORN CHOWDER

Microwave Cooking Time: 26 minutes   *4 servings*
Conventional Cooking Time: 32 minutes

1/2 pound bacon, diced	1/2 teaspoon pepper
1 onion, chopped	1 can (16 ounces)
2 stalks celery, sliced	cream-style corn
3 medium-size potatoes, diced (about 3 cups)	1 cup half-and-half
1 teaspoon salt	Chopped parsley for garnish

Microwave: Combine bacon, onion and celery in 3-quart glass bowl. Cover tightly with SARAN WRAP, turning back edge to vent. Microcook at 100% power 8 minutes, stirring once, until bacon is lightly browned. If desired, spoon off part of bacon drippings. Add potatoes, salt, pepper and 2 cups water. Recover, leaving vent, and microcook at 100% power 13 to 15 minutes, or until potatoes are tender, stirring once. Stir in corn and half-and-half. Recover and microcook at 70% power 5 minutes or until hot and bubbly. Let stand 5 minutes. Ladle into soup bowls and sprinkle with parsley.

Conventional: Sauté bacon, onion and celery in Dutch oven until onion is transparent. If desired, spoon off part of bacon drippings. Add potatoes, salt, pepper and 2 1/2 cups water. Heat to boiling. Reduce heat, cover and simmer 20 minutes or until potatoes are tender. Stir in corn and half-and-half. Heat 5 minutes or until hot and bubbly. Ladle into soup bowls and sprinkle with parsley.

CHERRY SOUP

Microwave Cooking Time: 25 minutes   *6 servings*
Conventional Cooking Time: 30 minutes

1 pound dark sweet cherries, pitted	3 tablespoons sugar
1 cup dry red wine	2 tablespoons cornstarch
1 lemon, sliced and seeded	2 tablespoons lemon juice
1 stick cinnamon	Lemon slices and dairy sour cream for garnish

Microwave: Combine cherries, wine, sliced lemon and cinnamon stick in 2 1/2-quart glass bowl or casserole. Cover tightly with SARAN WRAP, turning back edge to vent. Microcook at 100% power 7 minutes. Stir, recover, leaving vent, and microcook at 50% power 10 minutes. Cool slightly. Pour about half the mixture into blender or food processor. Blend until smooth. Transfer to bowl. Repeat with remaining cherry mixture. Mix sugar and cornstarch. Stir into cherry mixture. Cover tightly with SARAN WRAP, turning back edge to vent. Microcook at 100% power 8 minutes or until mixture boils, stirring 2 or 3 times. Add lemon juice and chill. Top servings with lemon slices and a dollop of sour cream.

Conventional: Combine cherries, wine, sliced lemon and cinnamon stick in 2-quart saucepan. Heat to boiling. Reduce heat, cover and simmer 20 minutes, stirring occasionally. Blend mixture as in microwave method, then return soup to saucepan. Combine sugar and cornstarch and stir into soup. Bring to a full rolling boil. Boil 1 minute. Chill. Top servings with lemon slices and a dollop of sour cream.

SPANISH CHICKEN SOUP

Microwave Cooking Time: 24 minutes   *6 servings*
Conventional Cooking Time: 30 minutes

1 can (10 3/4 ounces)
    condensed chicken
    broth, undiluted
1 can (16 ounces) stewed
    tomatoes
1 cup diced ham
1 boneless chicken breast
    (about 1/3 pound),
    diced
1/2 cup sliced pepperoni
1 onion, diced

2 cloves garlic, minced
    Vegetable oil (use in
    conventional method
    only)
2 teaspoons chili powder
1 package (10 ounces)
    frozen chopped spinach,
    partially thawed
1 can (16 ounces)
    garbanzo beans (chick
    peas), undrained

Microwave: Combine chicken broth, tomatoes, ham, chicken, pepperoni, onion, garlic, chili powder and 1 1/4 cups water in microsafe soup tureen. Cover tightly with SARAN WRAP, turning back edge to vent. Microcook at 100% power 14 minutes, stirring once. Add spinach and garbanzo beans. Recover, leaving vent, and microcook at 100% power 10 to 12 minutes or until spinach is cooked. Let stand, covered, 5 minutes. Ladle into bowls.

Conventional: Sauté ham, chicken, pepperoni, onion and garlic in 2 tablespoons vegetable oil in Dutch oven until lightly browned. Stir in chicken broth, tomatoes, chili powder and 2 cups water. Heat to boiling. Reduce heat, cover and simmer 15 minutes. Add spinach and garbanzo beans, cover and simmer 10 minutes longer. Ladle into bowls.

SUMMER SOUP

Microwave Cooking Time: 21 minutes   *6 servings*
Conventional Cooking Time: 35 minutes

4 cups chicken broth
1 carrot, sliced
1 onion, diced
2 sprigs parsley
1/4 teaspoon oregano
2 ears corn or 1 can
    (8 ounces) whole kernel
    corn, drained
1 1/2 cups cauliflowerettes
    (about 1/4 medium-
    size head)

1 cup fresh green beans,
    cut into 1-inch pieces
1 medium-size zucchini,
    sliced
2 tomatoes, cut into
    chunks
Salt and freshly ground
    pepper to taste
Chopped parsley for
    garnish

Microwave: Combine chicken broth, carrot, onion, parsley and oregano in 3-quart microsafe soup tureen or casserole. Cover tightly with SARAN WRAP, turning back edge to vent. Microcook at 100% power 6 minutes. Cut kernels from ears of corn. Add corn, cauliflower and green beans to soup. Recover, leaving vent, and microcook at 100% power 10 minutes. Add zucchini and tomatoes. Recover and microcook at 100% power 5 minutes. Season to taste with salt and pepper. Ladle into soup bowls and sprinkle with chopped parsley.

Conventional: Combine chicken broth, carrot, onion, parsley and oregano in large saucepan. Heat to boiling. Reduce heat, cover and simmer 10 minutes. Cut kernels from ears of corn. Add corn, cauliflower and green beans to soup. Cover and simmer 12 minutes. Stir in zucchini and tomatoes and simmer 5 minutes. Season to taste with salt and pepper. Serve as above.

Nice to know: A handful of fresh spinach, stirred into steaming soup just before serving, adds extra flavor. Sprinkle with Parmesan cheese and serve with crusty loaf of Italian bread for a fresh-from-the-garden summer dinner.

Summer Soup, Cherry Soup (page 24)

FRENCH ONION SOUP

Microwave Cooking Time: 25 minutes   *4 servings*
Conventional Cooking Time: 40 minutes

4 medium-size onions, sliced	2 cans (10 1/2 ounces each) condensed beef broth, undiluted
1/4 cup butter or margarine	
1/2 teaspoon thyme	4 thick slices French bread, toasted
3 tablespoons all-purpose flour	1 1/2 cups (6 ounces) shredded Swiss cheese

Microwave: Combine onions, butter and thyme in 3-quart glass mixing bowl. Cover tightly with SARAN WRAP, turning back edge to vent. Microcook at 100% power 8 minutes or until tender, stirring once. Stir in flour until smooth. Blend in 2 cups water and beef broth. Recover, leaving vent, and microcook at 100% power 14 minutes, stirring twice. Ladle soup over bread into four 2-cup microsafe crocks or bowls. Sprinkle with cheese. Microcook at 70% power 3 to 4 minutes or until cheese melts.

Conventional: Sauté onions in butter until onions are transparent, about 10 minutes. Stir in thyme and flour until blended. Add beef broth and 2 1/2 cups water. Stir until smooth. Heat to boiling. Reduce heat, cover and simmer 15 minutes. Preheat oven to 400°. Ladle soup over bread in ovenproof crocks or bowls. Sprinkle with cheese. Place bowls on cookie sheet and bake 15 minutes or until cheese is lightly browned.

FISH CHOWDER

Microwave Cooking Time: 33 minutes   *4 servings*
Conventional Cooking Time: 35 minutes

6 slices bacon	1/4 teaspoon pepper
1 medium-size onion, chopped	1 can (8 ounces) tomatoes
	1 pound fish fillets
2 stalks celery, diced	2 cups half-and-half
2 medium-size potatoes, cut into chunks	2 tablespoons chopped parsley
1/2 teaspoon thyme	Croutons
1 teaspoon salt	

Microwave: Combine bacon, onion and celery in 3-quart casserole. Cover tightly with SARAN WRAP, turning back edge to vent. Microcook at 100% power 8 minutes, stirring once. Add 2 cups water, potatoes, thyme, salt and pepper. Recover, leaving vent, and microcook at 100% power 12 minutes. Add tomatoes and fish. Recover and microcook at 100% power 7 minutes. Add half-and-half. Stir mixture gently to break fish into large flakes. Recover and microcook at 50% power 6 minutes, until just heated. Season to taste with salt and pepper. Ladle into soup bowls and sprinkle with parsley and croutons.

Conventional: Sauté bacon, onion and celery in Dutch oven until onion is transparent. Add 2 1/2 cups water, potatoes and seasonings. Heat to boiling. Reduce heat, cover and simmer 15 to 20 minutes or until potatoes are tender. Add tomatoes and fish. Cover and simmer 10 minutes. Add half-and-half. Stir gently to break fish into large flakes. Serve piping hot as above.

CHEDDAR CHEESE SOUP

Microwave Cooking Time: 16 minutes   *4 servings*
Conventional Cooking Time: 20 minutes

1/4 cup butter or margarine	1/2 teaspoon Worcestershire sauce
1 onion, minced	
1 carrot, minced	2 cups (8 ounces) shredded Cheddar cheese
1/2 stalk celery, minced	
3 tablespoons all-purpose flour	1 1/2 cups milk or half-and-half
2 cans (10 3/4 ounces each) condensed chicken broth, undiluted	Salt to taste
	Croutons
	Chopped parsley

Microwave: Combine butter, onion, carrot and celery in 2 1/2-quart glass bowl. Cover tightly with SARAN WRAP, turning back edge to vent. Microcook at 100% power 5 minutes, stirring once. Blend in flour until smooth. Blend in chicken broth and Worcestershire. Recover, leaving vent, and microcook at 100% power 5 minutes, stirring once. Gradually add cheese, stirring until smooth. Add milk and salt. Recover and microcook at 70% power 6 minutes or until steaming hot. Ladle into soup bowls and top with croutons and chopped parsley.

Conventional: Sauté onion, carrot and celery in butter in large saucepan. Stir in flour until smooth. Gradually add chicken broth and Worcestershire. Heat to simmering. Cover and simmer 10 minutes or until vegetables are tender. Stir in cheese until melted. Add milk and heat. Season with salt. Ladle into soup bowls and top with croutons and chopped parsley.

DILLED FISH SOUP

Microwave Cooking Time: 30 minutes　　　　　　　　　*4 servings*
Conventional Cooking Time: 38 minutes

    2 stalks celery, diced
    1 onion, chopped
    3 tablespoons butter or
        margarine
    4 medium-size potatoes,
        diced (about 4 cups)
    2 teaspoons dill
1 1/2 teaspoons salt
  1/2 teaspoon pepper
    1 pound cod or whitefish
        fillets

1 package (10 ounces)
    frozen French-cut
    green beans
1 package (10 ounces)
    frozen peas
Chopped parsley and
    dairy sour cream for
    garnish

Microwave:　Combine celery, onion and butter in 4-quart casserole. Cover tightly with SARAN WRAP, turning back edge to vent. Microcook at 100% power 3 minutes. Stir in 3 cups water, potatoes, dill, salt and pepper. Recover, leaving vent, and microcook at 100% power 12 minutes, stirring once. Cut fish into 1-inch cubes. Add to soup mixture with beans and peas. Recover and microcook at 100% power 15 minutes or until fish flakes easily, stirring once. Ladle into soup bowls and garnish with chopped parsley and a dollop of sour cream.

Conventional:　Sauté celery and onion in butter until onion is transparent and celery is tender. Add 3 1/2 cups water, potatoes, dill, salt and pepper. Heat to boiling. Reduce heat, cover and simmer 20 minutes. Add beans and peas and cook 5 minutes or until vegetables are thawed and soup is hot. Cut fish into 1-inch cubes. Add to soup and cook 5 to 8 minutes longer or until fish flakes easily. Serve as above.

Nice to know:　If you like creamy soup, add 1 cup half-and-half or heavy cream just before serving. Heat gently but do not boil.

OYSTER STEW

Microwave Cooking Time: 25 minutes   *4 servings*
Conventional Cooking Time: 44 minutes

4 cups half-and-half	1 1/4 teaspoons salt
1 onion, minced	1/4 teaspoon freshly ground
1/4 cup butter or	pepper
margarine	Oyster crackers or diced,
2 tablespoons all-purpose	buttered toast
flour	Chopped parsley for
2 cups shucked oysters,	garnish
undrained	
1 tablespoon	
Worcestershire sauce	

Microwave: Place half-and-half in 2-quart glass bowl. Microcook at 100% power 6 minutes or until steaming hot but not boiling. Cover with SARAN WRAP and set aside. Combine onion and butter in 3-quart glass bowl or casserole. Cover tightly with SARAN WRAP, turning back edge to vent. Microcook at 100% power 4 minutes. Stir in flour until smooth. Add oysters, Worcestershire, salt and pepper. Stir, recover, leaving vent, and microcook at 100% power 6 minutes or until edges of oysters begin to curl, stirring once. Add hot half-and-half. Recover, leaving vent, and microcook at 50% power 9 minutes to blend flavors. Ladle into soup bowls and sprinkle with oyster crackers and chopped parsley.

Conventional: Heat half-and-half in small saucepan over low heat until hot but not boiling, about 10 minutes. Cover and set aside. In large saucepan, sauté onion in butter until onion is transparent, about 5 minutes. Stir in flour until smooth. Cook 1 minute. Add oysters, Worcestershire, salt and pepper. Reduce heat to low, cover and cook 8 minutes or until edges of oysters begin to curl. Add half-and-half. Cover and simmer over very low heat 20 minutes to blend flavors. Serve as above.

Enticing Entrees

BAKED ZITI

Microwave Cooking Time: 20 minutes

Conventional Cooking Time: 35 minutes

6 servings

- 1 pound lean ground beef
- 1 onion, chopped
- 1 green pepper, chopped
- 1 can (16 ounces) whole tomatoes, cut up
- 1 can (8 ounces) tomato sauce
- 1 teaspoon Italian seasoning or 1/2 teaspoon each basil and oregano
- 1 1/2 teaspoons salt
- 1/4 teaspoon pepper
- 1/2 pound ziti or elbow macaroni, cooked and drained
- 1 package (8 ounces) mozzarella cheese, diced

Microwave: Break up meat into 2 1/2-quart casserole or glass bowl. Add onion and green pepper. Stir well to combine. Cover tightly with SARAN WRAP, turning back edge to vent. Microcook at 100% power 5 minutes, stirring once. Drain off excess fat. Add tomatoes, tomato sauce, Italian seasoning, salt and pepper. Stir to mix. Add ziti and half the cheese; stir well. Recover, leaving vent, and microcook at 70% power 12 minutes. Uncover, stir and sprinkle with remaining cheese. Microcook at 100% power 3 minutes. Let stand 5 minutes.

Conventional: Preheat oven to 350°. Sauté beef, onion and green pepper in large skillet until onion is transparent and meat is lightly browned. Drain off excess fat. Add tomatoes, tomato sauce, Italian seasoning, salt and pepper. Stir to mix. Add ziti and half the cheese; stir well. Spoon into 2 1/2-quart casserole and sprinkle with remaining cheese. Bake 25 to 30 minutes or until hot and bubbly and top is lightly browned.

STIR-FRIED BEEF AND PEPPERS

Microwave Cooking Time: 9 1/2 minutes   *4 servings*
Conventional Cooking Time: 13 minutes

5 tablespoons cooking oil, divided	3 tablespoons soy sauce
1 large green pepper, sliced	2 teaspoons cornstarch
1 large red pepper, sliced	1 teaspoon ginger
1 onion, sliced	1/8 teaspoon hot pepper sauce
3/4 pound beef flank steak, cut across the grain into very thin strips	Hot cooked rice

Microwave: Heat 10-inch square browning dish at 100% power 3 minutes. Add 3 tablespoons oil, green pepper, red pepper and onion. Stir well to coat with oil. Cover with glass lid and microcook at 100% power 3 minutes, stirring once. Remove vegetables from browning dish and set aside. Add remaining 2 tablespoons oil and meat to browning dish. Stir to coat meat with oil. Arrange meat in even layer and microcook, uncovered, 1 1/2 minutes. Blend soy sauce, 3 tablespoons water, cornstarch, ginger and hot pepper sauce. Pour over meat and stir to coat. Return vegetables to dish, cover with glass lid and microcook at 100% power 2 minutes, stirring once. Spoon into serving dish or over hot rice on warm platter and serve immediately. Pass additional soy sauce at table.

Conventional: Heat large skillet or Dutch oven over high heat 3 minutes. Add 3 tablespoons oil, green pepper, red pepper and onion. Cook, stirring constantly, until coated with oil. Stir-fry 5 minutes or until vegetables are tender-crisp. Remove vegetables from pan and set aside. Add remaining 2 tablespoons oil to skillet and heat. Add meat and stir-fry 3 minutes or until lightly browned. Mix soy sauce, 3 tablespoons water, cornstarch, ginger and hot pepper sauce. Pour over meat. Cook until sauce thickens and boils. Return vegetables to skillet and stir to coat. Serve as above.

Nice to know: Partially freeze meat for easy slicing. Flatten meat, cover with SARAN WRAP and freeze 15 to 30 minutes until meat is firm; then slice against grain with long sharp knife.

Steamed Chinese Bread (page 120),
Stir-Fried Beef and Peppers

SAUERBRATEN

Microwave Cooking Time: 1 hour, 27 minutes *8 servings*
Conventional Cooking Time: 3 hours, 15 minutes

2 cups red wine vinegar
1/2 cup dry red wine
1/4 cup firmly packed brown
    sugar
3 onions, sliced
12 peppercorns
12 whole cloves
2 teaspoons mustard seed
2 teaspoons salt
2 bay leaves
1 3-pound boneless beef
    chuck shoulder pot-roast
    or beef round bottom
    round roast

1/4 cup all-purpose flour
    (use in conventional
    method only)
3 tablespoons cooking oil
    (use in conventional
    method only)
1/2 cup gingersnap crumbs
1/2 cup dairy sour cream
    (optional)

Microwave: Combine vinegar, wine, brown sugar, onions, peppercorns, cloves, mustard seed, salt, bay leaves and 1 cup water in large microsafe bowl. Add meat, turning to coat with marinade. Cover tightly with SARAN WRAP and refrigerate 2 to 3 days, turning meat daily. When ready to cook, turn meat fat side down in marinade. Recover tightly with SARAN WRAP, turning back edge to vent. Microcook at 100% power 8 minutes. Reduce power to 50% and cook 1 hour 15 minutes to 1 hour 30 minutes, turning meat over after about 45 minutes. Lift meat from cooking liquid, place on warm platter and cover with SARAN WRAP. Strain cooking liquid, adding water if necessary to make up 2 1/2 cups. Combine liquid with gingersnap crumbs in 4-quart glass measure. Cover tightly with SARAN WRAP, turning back edge to vent. Microcook at 100% power 4 minutes, stirring twice. Blend in sour cream. Slice meat and spoon a little sauce over slices. Pass remaining sauce at table.

Conventional: Prepare meat as directed in microwave method. When ready to cook, remove meat from marinade. Pat dry with paper towels and coat with 1/4 cup flour. Heat oil in Dutch oven and brown meat well, about 10 minutes. Add marinade and heat to boiling. Reduce heat, cover and simmer 2 hours 30 minutes to 3 hours or until meat is fork-tender, turning meat over occasionally. Lift meat from cooking liquid, place on warm platter and cover with SARAN WRAP. Strain cooking liquid, adding water if necessary to make 2 1/2 cups. Combine liquid with gingersnap crumbs in saucepan. Heat to boiling, stirring constantly. Simmer 1 minute. Remove from heat and stir in sour cream. Serve as above.

MEATBALLS IN ITALIAN SAUCE

Microwave Cooking Time: 29 minutes   *4 servings*
Conventional Cooking Time: 40 minutes

Meatballs:

1 pound lean ground beef	1/2 teaspoon salt
1/2 cup dry bread crumbs	1/4 teaspoon freshly ground pepper
1/2 teaspoon oregano	

Sauce:

1 cup sliced mushrooms	1 tablespoon chopped fresh parsley
1 onion, finely chopped	1 teaspoon oregano
1/2 cup diced green pepper	1 teaspoon salt
3 tablespoons olive oil	1/4 teaspoon pepper
2 cans (16 ounces each) stewed tomatoes	1 bay leaf
1 can (6 ounces) tomato paste	1 pound spaghetti, cooked and drained
1/2 cup beef broth (use 1 cup in conventional method)	Grated Parmesan cheese

Microwave: Combine beef, bread crumbs, 1/2 teaspoon oregano, 1/2 teaspoon salt, 1/4 teaspoon pepper and 1/4 cup water. Mix well. Shape into 1-inch balls and place in 3-quart casserole. Cover tightly with SARAN WRAP, turning back edge to vent. Microcook at 100% power 6 minutes, stirring once. Drain off fat. Combine mushrooms, onion, green pepper and olive oil in glass bowl. Cover tightly with SARAN WRAP, turning back edge to vent. Microcook at 100% power 5 minutes. Add tomatoes, tomato paste, beef broth, parsley, 1 teaspoon oregano, 1 teaspoon salt, 1/4 teaspoon pepper and bay leaf. Mix well and pour over meatballs. Recover casserole, leaving vent, and microcook at 70% power 18 minutes, stirring once. Let stand 5 minutes, remove bay leaf and spoon over hot spaghetti. Sprinkle with Parmesan cheese and serve immediately.

Conventional: Prepare meatballs as directed in microwave method. Brown in 3 tablespoons oil in Dutch oven. Remove from pan and set aside. Place mushrooms, onion and green pepper in Dutch oven and sauté until onion is transparent, about 5 minutes. Stir in tomatoes, tomato paste, 1 cup beef broth, parsley, 1 teaspoon oregano, 1 teaspoon salt, 1/4 teaspoon pepper and bay leaf. Heat to boiling. Reduce heat, cover and simmer 20 minutes. Return meatballs to Dutch oven and cook 5 minutes longer to reheat meat. Remove bay leaf and serve as above.

CHILI

Microwave Cooking Time: 22 minutes　　　　　　　　　*8 servings*
Conventional Cooking Time: 40 minutes

2 pounds lean ground beef	3/4 teaspoon pepper
1 large onion, finely chopped	1 bay leaf
1 clove garlic, minced	2 cans (16 ounces each) kidney beans, drained
2 tablespoons chili powder	2 cans (16 ounces each) stewed tomatoes
2 teaspoons salt	

Microwave:　　Place beef, onion and garlic in 3-quart casserole. Mix to break up meat. Cover tightly with SARAN WRAP, turning back edge to vent. Microcook at 100% power 7 to 8 minutes or until meat loses pink color and onion is transparent. Stir once during cooking. Drain off excess fat. Stir in remaining ingredients. Recover, leaving vent and microcook at 100% power 15 to 20 minutes, stirring twice during cooking. Remove bay leaf and let stand, covered, 5 minutes before serving.

Conventional:　　In large skillet, sauté beef, onion and garlic until meat is lightly browned. Drain off excess fat. Stir in remaining ingredients and heat to just boiling. Reduce heat, cover, and simmer 30 minutes, stirring occasionally. Remove bay leaf and serve.

MOM'S MEATLOAF

Microwave Cooking Time: 28 minutes　　　　　　　*6 to 8 servings*
Conventional Cooking Time: 1 hour, 15 minutes

2 pounds lean ground beef	1 teaspoon oregano
1 cup fresh bread crumbs	1 tomato, sliced
1/2 cup minced onion	1 teaspoon browning sauce (microwave method only, optional)
1/2 cup milk	
1/4 cup ketchup	Fresh Tomato Sauce (page 102)
2 eggs, well-beaten	
2 teaspoons salt	
1/4 teaspoon freshly ground pepper	

Microwave:　　Combine meat, bread crumbs, onion, milk, ketchup, eggs, salt, pepper and oregano. Mix well. Spoon into 12 × 8-inch glass baking dish. Shape into 8 × 5-inch loaf, making ends square rather than oval. Mix browning sauce and 1-teaspoon water. Brush over meat. Arrange row of tomato slices along top of loaf. Cover tightly with SARAN WRAP, turning back edge to vent. Microcook at 70% power 28 to 30 minutes. Let stand 5 minutes. Lift out of baking dish and place on warm platter. Serve with Fresh Tomato Sauce.

Conventional: Preheat oven to 350°. Combine meat, bread crumbs, onion, milk, ketchup, eggs, salt, pepper and oregano. Mix well. Spoon into 12 × 8-inch baking pan and shape into 8 × 5-inch loaf. Arrange row of tomato slices along top of loaf. Bake 1 hour 15 minutes. Let stand 5 minutes. Serve as above.

MINI ROULADES

Microwave Cooking Time: 1 hour, 15 minutes   *8 servings*
Conventional Cooking Time: 2 hours, 10 minutes

1/2 cup all-purpose flour	1/4 cup chopped parsley
2 teaspoons salt, divided	2 large onions, sliced
1 teaspoon thyme, divided	3 tablespoons olive oil
1/2 teaspoon pepper	1 can (16 ounces) whole
2 1/2 pounds beef round	tomatoes, chopped
steak, cut 1/2-inch	1 can (10 1/2 ounces)
thick	condensed beef broth,
1/2 cup chopped celery	undiluted
leaves	

Microwave: Mix flour, 1 1/2 teaspoons salt, 1/2 teaspoon each thyme and pepper; coat meat. Pound coated meat with mallet until about 1/4-inch thick, adding as much flour mixture as possible. Sprinkle meat with celery leaves and half the parsley. Roll up and secure with wooden toothpicks, or tie with string. Set aside. Combine onions and oil in 3-quart round casserole. Cover tightly with SARAN WRAP, turning back edge to vent. Microcook at 100% power 5 minutes, stirring once. Add tomatoes, broth, remaining salt, thyme and parsley; stir lightly. Add reserved beef rolls; spoon a little sauce over meat. Recover, leaving vent, and microcook at 100% power 15 minutes. Rotate casserole; microcook at 50% power 55 to 60 minutes or until meat is fork-tender, rearranging rolls once. Let stand, covered, 10 minutes. Serve with sauce.

Conventional: Preheat oven to 325°. Prepare beef rolls as directed in microwave method. Set aside. In flameproof casserole, sauté onions in oil until transparent. Add tomatoes, broth and remaining seasonings. Heat to boiling. Add beef rolls, spooning a little sauce over meat. Cover tightly and bake 2 hours to 2 hours 30 minutes or until meat is fork-tender.

PASTITISO

Microwave Cooking Time: 55 1/2 minutes   *8 to 10 servings*
Conventional Cooking Time: 1 hour, 21 minutes

1 1/2 pounds lean ground beef
    1 large onion, minced
    1 can (8 ounces) tomato
        sauce
    1 can (6 ounces) tomato
        paste
1 1/2 teaspoons salt
  1/4 teaspoon pepper
    1 teaspoon oregano
  1/2 teaspoon cinnamon
    3 tablespoons butter or
        margarine

3 tablespoons all-purpose
   flour
2 1/2 cups milk (use 3 cups in
   conventional method)
3 egg yolks
1 pound elbow macaroni,
   cooked and drained
1 cup grated Parmesan
   cheese

Microwave: Grease 2 1/2-quart round casserole. Break meat into 4-quart glass bowl or casserole. Add onion and stir to mix. Cover tightly with SARAN WRAP, turning back edge to vent. Microcook at 100% power 9 minutes or until onion is tender and meat loses pink color, stirring twice. Drain off excess fat. Stir in tomato sauce, tomato paste, salt, pepper, oregano, cinnamon and 1/4 cup water. Recover, leaving vent, and microcook at 70% power 9 minutes. Place butter in 4-cup glass measure. Microcook at 100% power 1 1/2 minutes or until melted. Stir in flour; blend in milk; microcook at 100% power 6 minutes, stirring every other minute. Beat egg yolks. Gradually beat some hot milk mixture into yolks. Blend yolk mixture into sauce. Layer half macaroni in prepared casserole. Spoon half meat mixture over macaroni. Repeat layers once. Pour sauce over and sprinkle with cheese. Cover tightly with SARAN WRAP, turning back edge to vent. Microcook at 50% power 30 minutes, rotating casserole twice. Let stand, covered, 15 minutes before serving.

Conventional: Grease 2 1/2-quart casserole. Preheat oven to 350°. Sauté meat and onion in large skillet until meat is lightly browned and onion is transparent. Stir in tomato sauce, tomato paste, salt, pepper, oregano, cinnamon and 1/2 cup water. Cover and simmer 10 minutes. Melt butter in saucepan. Stir in flour until smooth. Cook 1 minute. Gradually blend in milk. Cook, stirring constantly, until sauce thickens. Beat egg yolks. Gradually beat some hot milk mixture into yolks. Blend yolk mixture into sauce. Layer half macaroni in prepared casserole. Spoon half meat mixture over macaroni. Repeat layers once.

Pour sauce over and sprinkle with cheese. Bake 55 to 60 minutes or until casserole is hot and lightly browned on top.

Nice to know: You can assemble most of this casserole in advance, but the egg yolk sauce should be made just before it is cooked. Microcooking and baking times must be increased slightly if the casserole is refrigerator temperature when it is placed in oven.

BEST-LOVED POT ROAST

Microwave Cooking Time: 1 hour, 9 minutes   *6 to 8 servings*
Conventional Cooking Time: 2 hours, 15 minutes

1 onion, sliced	1/2 teaspoon oregano
1 stalk celery, sliced	1/2 teaspoon thyme
2 tablespoons butter or margarine	1 teaspoon salt or to taste
1 2 1/2 to 3-pound boneless beef arm chuck roast	1/4 teaspoon freshly ground pepper
1 cup beef broth, vegetable broth, or water (use 1 1/2 cups in conventional method)	6 potatoes, peeled and halved
	6 carrots, cut into 1-inch chunks

Microwave: Combine onion, celery and butter in 4-quart casserole. Cover tightly with SARAN WRAP, turning back edge to vent. Microcook at 100% power 4 minutes. Add meat, broth, oregano, thyme, salt and pepper. Recover, leaving vent, and microcook at 100% power 5 minutes. Reduce power to 50% and microcook 20 minutes. Turn meat over, add potatoes, carrots and more liquid if necessary. Recover and microcook at 50% power 40 minutes longer or until meat is fork-tender, stirring twice. Let stand, covered, 5 minutes. Remove meat to warm platter. Carve thick slices and arrange vegetables around meat. Skim excess fat from cooking liquid, adjust seasoning and pour into sauceboat to serve at table.

Conventional: Sauté onion and celery in butter in Dutch oven. Push vegetables to one side. Add meat and brown lightly on each side. Stir in broth, oregano, thyme, salt and pepper. Heat to boiling. Reduce heat, cover and simmer 1 hour 30 minutes. Add potatoes, carrots and more liquid if necessary. Recover and simmer 30 minutes longer or until meat and vegetables are fork-tender. Remove meat to warm platter. Serve as above.

CREAMY SPINACH LASAGNA

Microwave Cooking Time: 40 minutes   *6 servings*
Conventional Cooking Time: 55 minutes

1   pound lean ground beef
1   onion, chopped
1/4 pound mushrooms, sliced
1/4 cup all-purpose flour
1/2 teaspoon basil
     Salt and freshly ground
       pepper
1   cup milk (use 1 1/2
       cups in conventional
       method)
1   can (8 ounces) tomato
       sauce
1   egg

1   package (10 ounces)
       frozen chopped
       spinach, thawed and
       squeezed dry
1   cup ricotta or creamy
       cottage cheese
1/2 pound lasagna noodles,
       cooked and drained
1/4 pound mozzarella cheese,
       sliced or shredded
1/4 cup grated Parmesan
       cheese

Microwave: Grease 12 × 8-inch glass baking dish. Break meat into 3-quart glass bowl or casserole. Add onion and mushrooms. Cover tightly with SARAN WRAP, turning back edge to vent. Microcook at 100% power 6 minutes or until onion is transparent and meat loses pink color, stirring once. Pour off excess fat. Add flour, basil, 1 teaspoon salt and 1/4 teaspoon pepper. Stir until well combined. Stir in milk and tomato sauce. Recover, leaving vent, and microcook at 90% power 10 minutes, stirring twice, until sauce is thickened. Beat egg and 1/2 teaspoon salt in separate bowl. Stir in spinach and ricotta.

To assemble lasagna, spoon 1/3 meat mixture into prepared baking dish. Layer half the lasagna noodles over meat. Top with spinach mixture, then 1/3 meat mixture, mozzarella, remaining lasagna noodles and remaining portion of meat mixture. Sprinkle with Parmesan cheese. Cover tightly with SARAN WRAP, turning back edge to vent. Microcook at 90% power 24 minutes or until bubbly and top is lightly browned, rotating dish twice during cooking. Let stand 10 minutes. Serve as above.

Conventional: Grease 12 × 8-inch or 13 × 9-inch baking dish. Preheat oven to 350°. Sauté meat, onion and mushrooms in large skillet until meat is lightly browned. Pour off excess fat. Stir in flour, basil, 1 teaspoon salt and 1/4 teaspoon pepper. Stir in 1 1/2 cups milk, tomato sauce and 1/2 cup water. Heat to boiling, stirring constantly. Remove from heat. Beat egg with 1/2 teaspoon salt. Stir in spinach and ricotta cheese. Assemble lasagna as directed in microwave method. Bake 40 to 45 minutes or until hot and bubbly. Let stand 10 minutes. Serve as above.

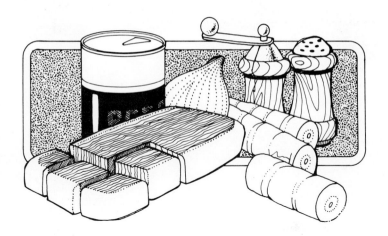

BEEF AND BEER STEW

Microwave Cooking Time: 54 minutes   *6 servings*
Conventional Cooking Time: 2 hours, 5 minutes

1 large onion, chopped	1 1/2 teaspoons salt
2 carrots, chopped	1/4 teaspoon pepper
2 tablespoons cooking oil	1/2 teaspoon thyme
2 pounds beef stew meat, cut into 1-inch cubes	1/2 teaspoon anise seed or caraway seed (optional)
1 cup beer (use 1 1/2 cups in conventional method)	1 bay leaf

Microwave: Combine onion, carrots and oil in 2 1/2-quart glass bowl or casserole. Cover tightly with SARAN WRAP, turning back edge to vent. Microcook at 100% power 4 minutes. Stir in meat, beer, salt, pepper, thyme, anise seed and bay leaf. Recover, leaving vent, and microcook at 100% power 5 minutes. Reduce power to 50% and microcook 45 minutes longer or until meat is fork-tender, stirring twice. Let stand 5 minutes. Remove bay leaf and serve over hot cooked noodles or rice.

Conventional: Sauté onion and carrots in oil in Dutch oven until onion is transparent, about 5 minutes. Stir in meat, 1 1/2 cups beer, salt, pepper, thyme, anise seed and bay leaf. Heat to boiling. Reduce heat, cover and simmer 2 hours or until meat is fork-tender, adding beer or water if necessary. Serve as above.

Nice to know: This stew can also be served as filling in a hot sandwich. Cut meat in 1/2-inch cubes and cook as directed. Spoon into warm pita bread halves and top with a dollop of sour cream. Serve with ice-cold beer or cider.

SWEET AND SOUR PORK

Microwave Cooking Time: 38 minutes   *4 to 6 servings*
Conventional Cooking Time: 1 hour, 30 minutes

1 can (20 ounces) pineapple chunks	2 pounds boneless pork, cut into 1-inch cubes
1/4 cup vinegar	1 large onion, cut into chunks
2 tablespoons soy sauce	1 large green pepper, cut into chunks
3 tablespoons cornstarch	Hot cooked rice
1 1/2 teaspoons salt	
1/4 teaspoon ginger	

Microwave: Drain juice from pineapple into 2 1/2-quart casserole. Add vinegar, soy sauce, cornstarch, salt and ginger. Stir until smooth. Add meat. Cover tightly with SARAN WRAP, turning back edge to vent. Microcook at 100% power 5 minutes. Stir, recover, leaving vent, and microcook at 70% power 25 minutes, stirring twice. Add onion, green pepper and pineapple chunks. Recover and microcook at 70% power 8 minutes or until pepper and onion are barely tender. Stir well and serve over rice.

Conventional: Drain juice from pineapple and place in Dutch oven. Add vinegar, soy sauce, salt, ginger and 1/2 cup water. Stir until smooth. Add meat and heat to boiling. Reduce heat, cover and simmer 1 hour 15 minutes or until meat is fork-tender. Add onion, green pepper and pineapple chunks. Simmer 10 minutes longer or until pepper and onion are barely tender. Blend cornstarch and 3 tablespoons water, stir into pan juices, heat to boiling and cook 1 minute. Serve over rice.

TAMALES

Microwave Cooking Time: 52 1/2 minutes　　　　　　　　*6 servings*
Conventional Cooking Time: 2 hours, 20 minutes

Meat Filling:

1 1/2 pounds boneless pork,
　　　cut into 1/2-inch cubes
　1 onion, chopped
　2 cloves garlic, minced
　2 tablespoons cooking oil
　　　(use in conventional
　　　method only)

　1 tablespoon chili powder
1 1/2 teaspoons oregano
1 1/2 teaspoons salt
　1 teaspoon cumin
　1/4 teaspoon cayenne

Tamale Paste:

1 1/4 cups beef broth
2 1/2 cups white cornmeal
　2 teaspoons salt
　2/3 cup shortening

12 corn husks, soaked 1
　　hour in hot water
　1 can (10 ounces) tamale
　　or enchilada sauce

Microwave: Combine meat, onion and garlic in 1 1/2-quart glass bowl or casserole. Cover tightly with SARAN WRAP, turning back edge to vent. Microcook at 100% power 5 minutes. Stir in chili powder, oregano, salt, cumin, cayenne and 2/3 cup water. Recover, leaving vent, and microcook at 70% power 30 minutes, stirring twice. Set aside to cool. Grind meat mixture in grinder or chop finely in food processor.

To make tamale paste, place beef broth in 2-cup glass measure. Cover tightly with SARAN WRAP, turning back edge to vent. Microcook at 100% power 2 1/2 minutes or until boiling. Mix cornmeal and salt. Cut in shortening until crumbly. Stir in beef broth to form thick paste.

Drain corn husks. Spread 3 tablespoons tamale paste down center of husks. Spoon 3 tablespoons meat mixture over tamale paste. Roll up husks loosely so paste encloses meat filling. Repeat with remaining ingredients. Tie ends of husks with string or thin strips of corn husk. Place tamales in 12 × 8-inch glass baking dish. Add 1 cup water. Cover tightly with SARAN WRAP, turning back edge to vent. Microcook at 100% power 3 minutes. Rotate dish and microcook at 70% power 12 minutes. Turn tamales over and rearrange once during cooking. Heat tamale sauce. Carefully unroll tamales and place on warm platter. Spoon sauce over and serve immediately.

Conventional: Sauté meat, onion and garlic in oil until pork loses pink color and onion is transparent, about 15 minutes. Add chili powder, oregano, salt, cumin, cayenne and 3/4 cup water.

Heat to boiling. Reduce heat, cover and simmer 1 hour. Set aside to cool. Grind meat in grinder or chop finely in food processor.

To make tamale paste, heat beef broth to boiling. Mix cornmeal and salt. Cut in shortening until crumbly. Stir in beef broth to form thick paste.

Drain corn husks and assemble tamales as directed in microwave method. In large Dutch oven bring about 1/2 inch water to a boil. Place tamales on rack over water. Cover and simmer about 1 hour. Add additional water as necessary. Heat tamale sauce and serve as above.

SPICY FRANK AND BEAN CASSEROLE

Microwave Cooking Time: 15 minutes   *6 servings*
Conventional Cooking Time: 35 minutes

1 large green pepper, cut into 1/2-inch pieces	1 can (8 ounces) tomato sauce
1 large onion, coarsely diced	2 tablespoons prepared mustard
2 tablespoons cooking oil (use in conventional method only)	2 teaspoons chili powder
1 can (16 ounces) baked beans, undrained	1 pound frankfurters, cut into 1/2-inch pieces
1 can (16 ounces) whole kernel corn, drained	3 slices American cheese, halved diagonally

Microwave: Combine green pepper and onion in 2-quart glass bowl or casserole. Cover tightly with SARAN WRAP, turning back edge to vent. Microcook at 100% power 3 minutes. Stir in beans, corn, tomato sauce, mustard and chili powder. Add frankfurters and stir to combine. Recover, leaving vent, and microcook at 90% power 11 minutes, stirring twice. Uncover and top with cheese. Microcook at 90% power 1 minute to melt cheese. Let stand 5 minutes before serving.

Conventional: Lightly grease 2-quart casserole. Preheat oven to 350°. Sauté green pepper and onion in oil in skillet until onion is transparent, about 5 minutes. Stir in beans, corn, tomato sauce, chili powder and mustard. Add frankfurters and stir to combine. Pour into prepared casserole. Bake 25 minutes or until hot and bubbly. Arrange cheese over top of casserole and bake 5 minutes longer to melt cheese and brown lightly. Serve immediately.

MOUSSAKA

Microwave Cooking Time: 50 minutes   *6 servings*
Conventional Cooking Time: 1 hour, 24 minutes

1 large eggplant (about
  1 1/2 pounds), halved
  lengthwise and cut
  into 1/4-inch slices
1/2 cup olive oil (about)
1 pound lean ground lamb
  or beef
1 onion, chopped
1 clove garlic, minced
1 can (8 ounces) tomato
  sauce

1/4 cup dry red wine (use
  1/2 cup in conventional
  method)
2 teaspoons dill
1 bay leaf
1 teaspoon salt
1/8 teaspoon cinnamon
  Dash freshly ground
  pepper
2 tablespoons dry bread
  crumbs

Custard Sauce:

2 tablespoons butter or
  margarine
3 tablespoons all-purpose
  flour (use 2 tablespoons
  in conventional
  method)

1/4 teaspoon salt
2 cups half-and-half
2 egg yolks
1/2 cup grated Parmesan
  cheese
  Nutmeg

Microwave: Grease 8-inch square glass baking dish. Place eggplant slices (preferably peeled) on broiler pan. Brush both sides with oil. Broil close to heat 4 minutes on each side or until lightly browned. Set aside. Break up meat; combine with onion and garlic in large glass bowl. Cover tightly with SARAN WRAP, turning back edge to vent. Microcook at 100% power 6 minutes, stirring once. Drain off excess fat. Add tomato sauce, 1/4 cup wine, dill, bay leaf, salt, cinnamon and pepper. Recover, leaving vent, and microcook at 70% power 10 minutes, stirring once. Remove bay leaf and stir in bread crumbs. Layer half eggplant slices in prepared baking dish. Cover with meat sauce, top with remaining eggplant slices and set aside.

To make custard sauce, place butter in 1-quart glass measure. Microcook at 100% power 1 minute. Stir in 3 tablespoons flour and salt until smooth. Blend in half-and-half. Cover tightly with SARAN WRAP, turning back edge to vent. Microcook at 100% power 5 minutes or until thickened, stirring twice. Beat egg yolks well. Add a little hot sauce to yolks, blend and pour egg-sauce mixture back into glass measure, stirring rapidly. Pour over eggplant. Sprinkle with cheese and nutmeg. Cover tightly with SARAN WRAP, turning back edge to vent. Microcook at 50% power 20 minutes, rotating twice. Let stand 10 minutes before serving.

Conventional: Grease 8-inch square baking dish. Place eggplant slices on broiler pan. Brush on both sides with oil. Broil close to heat 4 minutes on each side or until lightly browned. Set aside. Sauté meat, onion, and garlic in skillet until meat is lightly browned, about 8 minutes. Drain off excess fat. Stir in tomato sauce, 1/2 cup wine, dill, bay leaf, salt, cinnamon and pepper. Heat to boiling, reduce heat, cover and simmer 15 minutes. Remove bay leaf and stir in bread crumbs. Preheat oven to 325°. Layer half eggplant slices in prepared baking dish. Cover with meat sauce and top with remaining eggplant slices.

To make custard sauce, melt butter in saucepan. Stir in 2 tablespoons flour and 1/4 teaspoon salt. Blend in half-and-half. Cook, stirring constantly, over medium heat until thickened, about 5 minutes. Beat egg yolks well. Add a little hot sauce to yolks, blend and pour egg-sauce mixture back into saucepan, stirring rapidly. Pour over eggplant slices. Sprinkle with cheese and nutmeg. Bake 40 to 45 minutes or until custard is set. Let stand 10 minutes before serving.

COUNTRY-STYLE RIBS AND KRAUT

Microwave Cooking Time: 30 minutes   *4 to 6 servings*
Conventional Cooking Time: 1 hour, 30 minutes

3 pounds pork loin back ribs or country-style ribs, cut 1-inch thick
1 package (2 pounds) sauerkraut, drained
1/3 cup firmly packed brown sugar
1 apple, cored and chopped
1 onion, chopped
1 teaspoon caraway seed
1/4 teaspoon pepper
1 bay leaf
Prepared mustard

Microwave: Place ribs in 4-quart casserole. Cover tightly with SARAN WRAP, turning back edge to vent. Microcook at 70% power 12 minutes, rearranging meat once. Remove meat from casserole. Drain off juices and discard. Combine sauerkraut, brown sugar, apple, onion, caraway, pepper and bay leaf. Place in casserole and top with pork. Recover, leaving vent, and microcook at 70% power 18 to 20 minutes or until pork is well done, stirring sauerkraut and rearranging meat once. Let stand 10 minutes. Discard bay leaf, spoon into large serving bowl and serve with mustard.

Conventional: Brown ribs in large Dutch oven. Pour off drippings. Add 1/2 cup water and heat to boiling. Reduce heat, cover and simmer 20 minutes. Mix sauerkraut, brown sugar, apple, onion, caraway, pepper and bay leaf. Add to Dutch oven. Cover and simmer 1 hour or until meat is well done. Serve as above.

TROPICAL FRUIT AND HAM

Microwave Cooking Time: 29 minutes   *8 servings*
Conventional Cooking Time: 1 hour, 20 minutes

1 onion, chopped	1 cup shredded coconut
1 green pepper, chopped	2 bananas, cut into chunks
2 tablespoons butter or margarine	2 tablespoons brown sugar
1 1/2 teaspoons curry powder or to taste	2 tablespoons lemon juice
	1/4 teaspoon salt
1 can (20 ounces) pineapple chunks, drained	1 3-pound canned ham
	Parsley sprigs for garnish

Microwave: Combine onion, green pepper, butter and curry powder in glass mixing bowl. Cover tightly with SARAN WRAP, turning back edge to vent. Microcook at 100% power 5 minutes, stirring once. Stir in pineapple, coconut, bananas, brown sugar, lemon juice and salt. Place ham in glass baking dish. Spoon fruit mixture over ham. Microcook at 70% power 24 minutes or until internal temperature of ham reaches 140°. Cover tightly with SARAN WRAP and let stand 5 minutes. Lift ham and fruit onto serving platter and garnish with parsley.

Conventional: Preheat oven to 325°. Place ham on rack in roasting pan. Bake 1 hour. Meanwhile, sauté onion, green pepper and curry powder in butter until onion is transparent. Remove from heat and stir in remaining ingredients. Spoon over ham. Bake 20 minutes longer or until internal temperature of ham reaches 140°. Serve as above.

Nice to know: You can assemble Moussaka for future use; follow steps as directed, cover tightly with SARAN WRAP and freeze. When ready to use, thaw covered Moussaka at 30% power 25 minutes, rotating once. Let stand 10 minutes. Microcook, covered, at 70% power 25 minutes, rotating twice. Let stand 10 minutes. Uncover and microcook at 100% power 6 minutes or until hot and bubbly.

Moussaka (page 48)

FRUIT-STUFFED PORK LOIN

Microwave Cooking Time: 33 minutes   6 to 8 servings
Conventional Cooking Time: 2 hours

1 **3-pound boneless rolled pork loin**	1/3 **cup orange juice, chicken broth or water**
1/2 **teaspoon salt and pepper**	1 **egg, beaten**
1 1/2 **cups fresh bread crumbs**	1/2 **teaspoon thyme**
1/2 **cup chopped raisins**	**Dash cinnamon**
2 **tablespoons chopped dried apricots**	**Apricot Sauce (page 104)**

Microwave: Cut strings and unroll meat. Place fat side down on cutting board and sprinkle lightly with salt and pepper. Combine bread crumbs, raisins, apricots, orange juice, egg, thyme, 1/2 teaspoon salt, pepper and cinnamon. Stir until evenly moistened. Spoon onto meat. Reroll meat and retie firmly with string. Place meat on microsafe rack in shallow microsafe roasting pan. Cover tightly with SARAN WRAP, turning back edge to vent. Microcook at 70% power 10 minutes. Uncover and turn meat over. Brush with Apricot Sauce. Microcook, uncovered, at 70% power 23 to 25 minutes longer or until microsafe meat thermometer reads 160°, brushing with sauce once more. Let stand, covered with SARAN WRAP, 10 minutes. Carve thick slices and serve with additional warmed Apricot Sauce.

Conventional: Preheat oven to 325°. Stuff, roll and tie meat as directed in microwave method. Place meat on rack in roasting pan. Roast 2 hours or until meat thermometer reaches 160°. Brush with Apricot Sauce during last 30 minutes of roasting. Let stand 10 minutes. Serve as above.

Cinnamon-Apple Sweet Potatoes (page 96),
Apricot Sauce (page 104), Fruit-Stuffed Pork Loin

VEAL PAPRIKASH

Microwave Cooking Time: 43 minutes　　　　　　　*6 servings*
Conventional Cooking Time: 1 hour, 7 minutes

2 onions, coarsely chopped	2 1/4 teaspoons salt
1/4 cup butter or margarine	1/2 cup dry vermouth
1 to 2 tablespoons paprika	1/2 cup dairy sour cream
2 pounds veal for stew, cut into 1-inch cubes	Hot cooked noodles
1/4 cup all-purpose flour	Chopped parsley for garnish

Microwave: Combine onions, butter and paprika in 2-quart glass bowl or casserole. Cover tightly with SARAN WRAP, turning back edge to vent. Microcook at 100% power 4 minutes. Coat meat with flour and salt and add to onions. Add vermouth, recover, leaving vent, and microcook at 100% power 4 minutes. Stir well, recover and microcook at 50% power 35 minutes or until meat is fork-tender, stirring twice. Let stand, covered, 5 minutes. Blend in sour cream and spoon over noodles on large warm platter. Sprinkle with parsley and serve immediately.

Conventional: Sauté onions in butter until onions are transparent, about 5 minutes. Stir in paprika and cook 1 to 2 minutes longer. Coat meat with flour and salt and add to pan. Add 3/4 cup water or chicken broth and heat to simmering. Cover and simmer 1 hour or until meat is fork-tender. Serve as above.

LUAU CHICKEN

Microwave Cooking Time: 30 minutes　　　　　　*4 to 6 servings*
Conventional Cooking Time: 50 minutes

1 3-pound broiler/fryer, cut up	2 tablespoons lemon juice
1/4 cup all-purpose flour	1/8 teaspoon cloves
1 1/2 teaspoons salt	1 can (20 ounces) crushed pineapple
1/4 teaspoon pepper	1/2 cup golden raisins
3/4 teaspoon ginger	1/2 cup orange juice (use in conventional method only)
3 tablespoons butter or margarine (use in conventional method only)	2 oranges, sectioned
2 tablespoons cornstarch	Toasted sliced almonds for garnish

Microwave: Wash chicken and pat dry. Mix flour, salt, pepper and ginger. Coat chicken pieces with flour mixture and arrange in 4-quart casserole, placing thickest pieces at edge of dish. Cover tightly with SARAN WRAP, turning back edge to vent. Microcook at 100% power 15 minutes. Blend cornstarch, lemon juice and cloves until smooth. Stir in pineapple and raisins. Rearrange chicken pieces and pour pineapple mixture over. Top with orange sections. Recover, leaving vent, and microcook at 100% power 15 minutes or until tender. Let stand, covered, 5 minutes. Place chicken on warm platter and sprinkle with toasted almonds.

Conventional: Coat chicken pieces with flour mixture as above. Brown in 3 tablespoons butter in large skillet about 10 minutes. Blend cornstarch, lemon juice and cloves until smooth. Stir in pineapple, raisins and 1/2 cup orange juice. Pour over chicken. Cover and simmer 40 minutes or until fork-tender. Top with orange slices and toasted almonds.

CHICKEN CACCIATORE

Microwave Cooking Time: 35 minutes   *6 servings*
Conventional Cooking Time: 55 minutes

1	large onion, chopped	2	teaspoons salt
1	large green pepper, chopped	1/2	teaspoon pepper
3	cloves garlic, minced	1	bay leaf
1/4	cup olive oil	1	3-pound broiler/fryer, cut up
1	can (28 ounces) stewed tomatoes	1/2	cup dry red wine (use 1 cup in conventional method)
2	teaspoons oregano		

Microwave: Combine onion, green pepper, garlic and olive oil in 2-quart glass bowl. Cover tightly with SARAN WRAP, turning back edge to vent. Microcook at 100% power 5 minutes, stirring once. Stir in tomatoes, wine, oregano, salt, pepper and bay leaf. Arrange chicken in 4-quart casserole, placing thicker pieces at edge of dish. Pour tomato mixture over chicken. Cover tightly wtih SARAN WRAP, turning back edge to vent. Microcook at 100% power 30 to 35 minutes or until chicken is fork-tender, rotating casserole twice. Discard bay leaf and let stand, covered, 5 minutes. Place chicken and sauce in serving dish and serve with hot cooked spaghetti or ziti.

Conventional: Heat olive oil in 12-inch skillet. Brown chicken in oil, about 10 minutes. Remove chicken from skillet. Add onion, green pepper and garlic and sauté until onion is transparent. Stir in tomatoes, wine, oregano, salt, pepper and bay leaf. Nestle chicken in sauce and heat to boiling. Reduce heat, cover and simmer 40 minutes or until chicken is fork-tender. Discard bay leaf and serve as above.

DIJON-TARRAGON CHICKEN

Microwave Cooking Time: 16 minutes   *6 servings*
Conventional Cooking Time: 33 minutes

1 onion, thinly sliced	1 teaspoon tarragon
1/4 cup butter or margarine	1/2 teaspoon salt
3 large chicken breasts, boned, skinned, and halved	1/4 teaspoon freshly ground pepper
1/2 cup heavy cream (use 1 cup in conventional method)	1/2 cup dairy sour cream Watercress, parsley or fresh tarragon for garnish
2 tablespoons Dijon-style mustard	

Microwave: Place onion and butter in 12 × 8-inch glass baking dish. Cover tightly with SARAN WRAP, turning back edge to vent. Microcook at 100% power 5 minutes. Add chicken breasts, turning over to coat with butter. Recover, leaving vent, and microcook at 100% power 6 minutes. Rearrange chicken, placing uncooked sections close to edge of dish. Mix heavy cream, mustard, tarragon, salt and pepper until smooth. Pour over chicken. Recover and microcook at 70% power 5 to 6 minutes or until chicken is fork-tender. Lift chicken to warm serving platter. Using whisk, blend sour cream into gravy until smooth. Spoon over chicken, garnish and serve immediately.

Conventional: Heat butter in large skillet. Add chicken breasts and brown lightly on each side over low heat, about 8 minutes. Remove chicken from skillet. Add onion and sauté until onion is transparent, about 5 minutes. Stir in 1 cup heavy cream, mustard, tarragon, salt and pepper. Add chicken and heat to simmering. Cover and simmer gently until chicken is fork-tender, about 20 minutes. Remove chicken from skillet. Using whisk, blend sour cream into gravy until smooth. Spoon over chicken, garnish and serve immediately.

Menu Hint: Serve this company main dish with a salad of Belgian endive, Asparagus Vinaigrette (page 86), parslied rice and Strawberry Rhubarb Soufflé (page 143).

JAMBALAYA

Microwave Cooking Time: 46 minutes　　　　　　　　　　*6 servings*
Conventional Cooking Time: 55 minutes

1 large onion, chopped	2 teaspoons thyme
1 green pepper, chopped	2 teaspoons salt
1 stalk celery, chopped	1/2 teaspoon pepper
2 cloves garlic, minced	1/4 teaspoon hot pepper
1/2 cup diced ham	sauce
1/4 cup olive oil	1 2 1/2 pound broiler/
1 can (28 ounces) stewed	fryer, cut up
tomatoes	Paprika
1 1/3 cups chicken broth	1 pound shrimp, cleaned
1 cup instant rice	

Microwave: Combine onion, green pepper, celery, garlic, ham and oil in 4-quart casserole. Cover tightly with SARAN WRAP, turning back edge to vent. Microcook at 100% power 8 minutes, stirring once. Stir in tomatoes, chicken broth, rice, thyme, salt, pepper and hot pepper sauce. Sprinkle chicken with paprika. Add to casserole, placing thicker pieces at edge of dish. Recover, leaving vent, and microcook at 100% power 35 minutes, stirring once. Add shrimp and stir to combine. Recover and microcook at 70% power 3 minutes. Let stand 5 minutes.

Conventional: Rub chicken with paprika. Brown chicken in olive oil in large skillet. Remove chicken from pan. Add onion, green pepper, celery and garlic. Sauté until onion is transparent, about 10 minutes. Stir in ham, tomatoes, chicken broth, rice and seasonings. Add chicken and spoon sauce over. Heat to boiling. Reduce heat, cover and simmer 30 minutes or until chicken is tender. Stir in shrimp. Cook just until shrimp turns pink, about 3 minutes.

Nice to know:　You may use long grain rice in the conventional method, but increase chicken broth (or add water) to make 2 cups.

Freezer tip:　When you buy extra cut-up chickens, wrap each piece of chicken in SARAN WRAP, then over-wrap all the pieces with SARAN WRAP and freeze. To thaw, place individually wrapped pieces of chicken on tray of microwave oven and microcook at 30% power 18 to 20 minutes.

CHICKEN ENCHILADAS

Microwave Cooking Time: 26 minutes   *6 servings*
Conventional Cooking Time: 46 minutes

1 large onion, chopped	1 1/4 teaspoons salt
2 tablespoons butter or margarine	1/4 teaspoon hot pepper sauce
2 cups diced, cooked chicken	1 can (10 ounces) hot or mild enchilada sauce
1 cup creamy cottage cheese	1 cup cooking oil
1 can (4 ounces) green chilies, diced	12 soft corn tortillas
1/4 cup diced pimiento	2 cups shredded Monterey Jack or Cheddar cheese

Microwave: Combine onion and butter in 2-quart glass bowl or casserole. Cover tightly with SARAN WRAP, turning back edge to vent. Microcook at 100% power 4 minutes. Stir in chicken, cottage cheese, chilies, pimiento, salt and hot pepper sauce. Set aside. Place enchilada sauce in 8-inch round glass cake dish or pie plate. Cover tightly with SARAN WRAP, turning back edge to vent. Microcook at 100% power 2 minutes or until hot.

Heat oil in 10-inch skillet. Fry tortillas, one at a time, 20 to 30 seconds or until blistered and lightly browned. Drain on paper towels. Dip tortillas in enchilada sauce to coat. Spoon 1/3 cup chicken filling onto center of tortilla. Roll up tightly and place, seam-side down, in 12 × 8-inch microsafe baking dish. Repeat with remaining tortillas, sauce and filling. Drizzle remaining enchilada sauce over tortillas, moistening any dry surface. Cover tightly with SARAN WRAP, turning back edge to vent. Microcook at 90% power 12 minutes, rotating dish once. Uncover and sprinkle with cheese. Microcook at 100% power 2 minutes or until cheese melts.

Conventional: Preheat oven to 350°. Sauté onion in butter until onion is transparent, about 5 minutes. Remove from heat and stir in chicken, cottage cheese, chilies, pimiento, salt and hot pepper sauce. Set aside. Heat enchilada sauce in 9-inch skillet until hot. Remove from heat.

Prepare and fill tortillas as directed in microwave method. Roll up tightly and place, seam-side down, in 13 × 9-inch baking dish. Drizzle remaining enchilada sauce over tortillas, moistening any dry surface. Bake 25 to 30 minutes or until hot. Sprinkle with cheese and bake 5 minutes longer or until cheese melts.

Mexican Pepper Salad (page 96), Chicken Enchiladas

DUCKLING A L'ORANGE

Microwave Cooking Time: 46 minutes   *4 servings*
Conventional Cooking Time: 2 hours, 35 minutes

1 **5-pound duckling**	1 **tablespoon lemon juice**
Salt and freshly ground	1 **tablespoon cornstarch**
pepper	1/2 **teaspoon browning sauce**
1/2 **cup orange juice**	**(optional)**
Grated peel of 1 orange	2 **tablespoons brandy**
1/2 **cup dry white wine**	**Orange slices or wedges**
1/3 **cup sugar**	**Parsley sprigs**
2 **tablespoons orange-**	
flavored liqueur	

Microwave: Rinse duckling well. Sprinkle with salt and pepper. Prick skin in several places to allow fat to drain during cooking. Place duckling, breast side down, on microsafe rack in microsafe roasting pan. Cover tightly with SARAN WRAP, turning back edge to vent. Microcook at 70% power 20 minutes, rotating dish once. Turn duckling breast side up. Microcook, uncovered, at 70% power 14 to 16 minutes longer or until microsafe meat thermometer reads 185° when inserted in thickest part of breast or in joint between thigh and body. Preheat broiler. Cut duckling into quarters. Broil, skin side up, 8 to 10 minutes or until well-browned. Meanwhile, combine orange juice, orange peel, wine, sugar, liqueur, lemon juice, cornstarch and browning sauce in 2-cup glass measure. Cover tightly with SARAN WRAP, turning back edge to vent. Microcook at 100% power 4 minutes, stirring twice. Stir in brandy. Place duckling on platter and spoon a little sauce over. Place remaining sauce in sauceboat to pass at table. Garnish with orange slices or wedges and parsley sprigs.

Conventional: Preheat oven to 350°. Rinse duckling well. Sprinkle with salt and pepper. Prick skin in several places to allow fat to drain during cooking. Place duckling on rack in roasting pan. Roast 2 hours to 2 hours 30 minutes or until meat thermometer reads 185°. Meanwhile, combine orange juice, orange peel, wine, sugar, liqueur, lemon juice, cornstarch and browning sauce in small saucepan. Heat to boiling, stirring constantly. Boil 1 minute. Stir in brandy. Cut duckling into quarters, place on platter and spoon a little sauce over. Place remaining sauce in sauceboat to pass at table. Garnish with orange slices or wedges and parsley sprigs.   ·

Nice to know: If you don't have a meat thermometer you can test for doneness by piercing duckling in thick joint between thigh and body. When duckling is done, juices will run clear. Do not use meat thermometer in microwave oven unless it is especially designed for microwave use. If your microwave oven has a meat probe, set probe at 185°.

CASSOULET

Microwave Cooking Time: 39 minutes   *6 servings*
Conventional Cooking Time: 1 hour, 15 minutes

1/2 cup diced salt pork or 6 slices bacon, diced	1/2 teaspoon thyme
1 onion, diced	1/8 teaspoon allspice
1 clove garlic, minced	1 bay leaf
2 boneless chicken breasts (about 3/4 pound), cut into 1-inch chunks	1/4 teaspoon pepper
	1 can (16 ounces) white beans, undrained
1/2 pound kielbasa or other fully cooked smoked sausage, cut into 1/2-inch pieces	1 can (8 ounces) tomato sauce
	1/2 cup dry vermouth
	Salt to taste
	Parsley for garnish

Microwave: Place salt pork in 4-quart casserole. Cover tightly with SARAN WRAP, turning back edge to vent. Microcook at 100% power 5 minutes or until browned. Add onion and garlic, recover, leaving vent, and microcook at 100% power 4 minutes longer. Add chicken, sausage, thyme, allspice, bay leaf and pepper. Recover and microcook at 70% power 5 minutes. Stir in beans, tomato sauce and vermouth. Recover and microcook at 50% power 25 minutes, stirring twice. Let stand 5 minutes. Remove bay leaf, season to taste with salt and garnish with parsley.

Conventional: Preheat oven to 375°. Sauté salt pork in saucepan until lightly browned. Add onion and garlic and sauté until onion is transparent. Add 1/2 cup water, chicken, sausage, thyme, allspice, bay leaf, pepper, beans, tomato sauce and vermouth. Heat to boiling. Season lightly with salt and pour into 2-quart casserole. Bake 1 hour, stirring once. Remove bay leaf, season to taste with salt and garnish with parsley.

Nice to know: Cassoulet is a simple French dish that has many variations. It can be made by substituting pork or veal for the chicken and substituting ham for the sausage. Serve in deep bowls with a crusty French bread and red wine.

TURKEY AND PILAF

Microwave Cooking Time: 58 minutes   *8 servings*
Conventional Cooking Time: 2 hours, 5 minutes

1 **5-pound frozen turkey breast, completely thawed**	1 **can (10 3/4 ounces) condensed chicken broth, undiluted**
1/4 **cup butter or margarine**	1 1/2 **teaspoons thyme**
1 **medium-size onion, chopped**	1 **teaspoon salt**
1/2 **pound mushrooms, sliced**	1/4 **teaspoon pepper**
2 **cups long grain rice**	1/2 **cup dry white wine**

Microwave: Place turkey breast, skin side down, in deep 4-quart casserole. Cover tightly with SARAN WRAP, turning back edge to vent. Microcook at 100% power 20 minutes. In glass bowl, combine butter, onion and mushrooms. Cover tightly with SARAN WRAP, turning back edge to vent. Microcook at 100% power 5 minutes, stirring twice. Add rice, recover, leaving vent, and microcook at 100% power 3 minutes. Stir in broth, thyme, salt, pepper and wine. Turn turkey skin side up. Pour rice mixture around turkey. Recover, leaving vent, and microcook at 70% power 30 to 35 minutes or until internal temperature reaches 175°. Stir rice and rotate casserole once during cooking. Let stand, covered, 5 minutes before serving.

Conventional: Preheat oven to 325°. Sauté mushrooms and onion in butter in skillet until onion is transparent. Add rice and cook, stirring, until rice is lightly browned. Stir in chicken broth, thyme, salt, pepper, wine and 3/4 cup water. Place turkey breast, skin side up, in deep 4-quart casserole. Pour rice mixture around turkey breast. Cover tightly and bake 2 hours or until internal temperature reaches 180°. Let stand 15 minutes before serving.

SWISS VEAL ROAST

Microwave Cooking Time: 1 hour, 5 minutes   *6 servings*
Conventional Cooking Time: 2 hours, 35 minutes

2 leeks, finely chopped
2 carrots, finely chopped
2 tablespoons butter or
    margarine (use 1/4 cup
    in conventional method)
1 3-pound boneless veal
    rump roast or shoulder
    roast with thin fat
    covering if possible
1 teaspoon salt
1/2 teaspoon pepper
1/4 teaspoon nutmeg

3 slices Swiss cheese,
    halved
3 slices boiled ham,
    halved or 6 thin
    slices Virginia ham
1/4 pound mushrooms, sliced
1/2 cup dry white wine (use
    1 cup in conventional
    method)
1/2 cup heavy cream
    (optional)
    Parsley for garnish

Microwave: Combine leeks, carrots and butter in 4-quart casserole. Cover tightly with SARAN WRAP, turning back edge to vent. Microcook at 100% power 5 minutes, stirring once. Meanwhile, make 6 deep cuts in roast, slicing about 3/4 of the way through. Sprinkle cut surfaces with salt, pepper and nutmeg. Tuck a piece of cheese and ham in each cut, and tie meat lengthwise with string. Place meat, cut side down, in casserole. Add mushrooms and wine. Cover tightly with SARAN WRAP, turning back edge to vent. Microcook at 70% power 25 minutes. Turn roast over, recover, leaving vent, and microcook at 70% power 35 to 40 minutes longer or until meat is fork-tender, rotating casserole once. If ends of roast begin to overcook, shield with foil. Lift roast from cooking liquid and let stand 10 minutes before carving.

To make sauce, skim excess fat from cooking liquid. Place skimmed cooking liquid and vegetables in blender and process until smooth. Add warm cream if desired. To serve, slice roast and garnish with parsley. Pass sauce separately.

Conventional: Preheat oven to 325°. Sauté leeks, carrots and 1/4 cup butter in flame-proof casserole until vegetables are tender, about 5 minutes. Make 6 deep cuts in roast, slicing about 3/4 of the way through. Sprinkle cut surfaces with salt, pepper and nutmeg. Tuck a piece of cheese and ham in each cut, and tie meat lengthwise with string. Place meat in casserole with mushrooms, 1 cup wine and 1/2 cup water. Heat to boiling. Cover and bake 2 hours to 2 hours 30 minutes or until meat is fork-tender. Lift roast from cooking liquid and let stand 10 minutes before carving. Prepare sauce as directed in microwave method and serve as above.

LIVER CREOLE

Microwave Cooking Time: 35 minutes   *4 to 6 servings*
Conventional Cooking Time: 45 minutes

1 onion, sliced	1 1/4 teaspoons salt, divided
1 green pepper, sliced	2 tablespoons all-purpose
2 stalks celery, sliced	flour
1 clove garlic, minced	1/2 teaspoon chili powder
4 slices bacon, diced	1/2 teaspoon thyme
1 can (16 ounces) stewed	1/4 teaspoon pepper
tomatoes	1 pound beef liver, cut
1 package (10 ounces)	into strips
frozen sliced okra	Hot cooked rice
1 bay leaf	

Microwave: Place onion, green pepper, celery, garlic and bacon in 4-quart casserole. Cover tightly with SARAN WRAP, turning back edge to vent. Microcook at 100% power 8 minutes, stirring once. Add tomatoes, okra, bay leaf, 1/4 teaspoon salt and 1/2 cup water. Recover, leaving vent, and microcook at 100% power 13 minutes. Mix flour, chili powder, thyme, pepper and remaining 1 teaspoon salt. Use to coat liver. Add liver to tomato mixture. Recover and microcook at 70% power 14 minutes, stirring twice, until liver is fork-tender. Remove bay leaf, taste and adjust seasoning if necessary. Serve with hot cooked rice.

Conventional: Sauté onion, green pepper, celery, garlic and bacon in large skillet until onion is transparent, about 10 minutes. Add tomatoes, okra, bay leaf, 1/4 teaspoon salt and 1 cup water. Heat to boiling. Reduce heat, cover and simmer 15 minutes. Mix flour, chili powder, thyme, pepper and remaining 1 teaspoon salt. Use to coat liver. Add liver to tomato mixture. Cover and simmer 15 minutes, or until liver is fork-tender. Serve as above.

Nice to know: If you want to use a special pottery baking dish in your microwave oven, test it first. Fill a 1-cup glass measure with water. Set glass measure in pottery dish and place in microwave oven. Microcook at 100% power 1 minute. If the dish is cool at the end of 1 minute, it is safe to use in the microwave oven. If it is warm or hot, it is absorbing microwave energy and should not be used. You can test any dish or bowl you own this way.

ORANGE HALIBUT STEAK

Microwave Cooking Time: 14 minutes   *4 to 6 servings*
Conventional Cooking Time: 24 minutes

3 tablespoons butter or margarine	Freshly ground pepper
1 1 1/2-pound halibut steak, cut about 1 1/2-inches thick	1/2 cup heavy cream or half-and-half
1/2 cup orange juice	2 tablespoons orange-flavored liqueur
1 teaspoon cornstarch	2 oranges, sectioned
Salt	Watercress or parsley sprigs for garnish

Microwave: Place butter in 2-cup glass measure. Microcook at 100% power 1 minute to melt. Place halibut steak on microsafe rack in 10 × 6-inch glass baking dish. Spoon 2 tablespoons melted butter over fish, reserving remainder of butter. Cover tightly with SARAN WRAP, turning back edge to vent. Microcook at 100% power 9 minutes, rotating dish once. Let stand, covered, while preparing sauce. Add orange juice, cornstarch, 1/2 teaspoon salt and dash pepper to remaining tablespoon butter in glass measure. Cover tightly with SARAN WRAP, turning back edge to vent. Microcook at 100% power 3 minutes, stirring twice. Stir in heavy cream and liqueur. Lift fish from cooking dish with slotted spatulas and place on microsafe serving platter. (If desired, carefully remove center bone and bony portions at pointed ends of fish.) Pour about half the sauce over and around fish. Sprinkle lightly with salt and pepper and arrange orange sections over fish. Microcook at 100% power 1 minute to heat orange sections. Garnish with watercress and serve immediately. Pass remaining sauce in sauceboat at table.

Conventional: Lightly grease small roasting pan. Preheat oven to 350°. Place fish in roasting pan. Melt butter in small saucepan. Spoon about 2 tablespoons butter over fish, reserving remainder of butter. Bake 15 to 20 minutes or until fish flakes easily. Add orange juice, cornstarch, 1/2 teaspoon salt and dash pepper to remaining tablespoon butter in saucepan. Stir until smooth. Heat to boiling, stirring constantly. Boil 1 minute. Stir in cream and liqueur. Heat gently until warm. Lift fish from roasting pan with slotted spatulas and place on warm serving platter. (If desired, carefully remove center bone and bony portions at pointed ends of fish.) Pour about half the sauce over and around fish. Sprinkle lightly with salt and pepper and arrange orange sections over fish. Garnish with watercress and serve immediately. Pass remaining sauce in sauceboat at table.

SHRIMP MOUSSE

Microwave Cooking Time: 7 1/2 minutes　　　　　*6 servings*
Conventional Cooking Time: 12 minutes

2 envelopes unflavored gelatin	2 tablespoons minced onion
3 tablespoons lemon juice	1/2 teaspoon dill
1 teaspoon salt	1 1/4 cups dairy sour cream
1 pound shrimp, peeled and cleaned	1/2 cup mayonnaise
1 cup finely chopped celery	1/4 cup chopped parsley
	Lettuce leaves
	Lemon wedges

Microwave:　Sprinkle gelatin over 1 cup cold water in 4-cup glass measure or casserole. Let stand 3 minutes to soften. Stir in lemon juice and salt. Cover tightly with SARAN WRAP, turning back edge to vent. Microcook at 100% power 3 minutes or until boiling. Add shrimp, recover, leaving vent, and microcook at 100% power 1 1/2 minutes. Let stand, covered, 3 minutes. Remove shrimp from cooking liquid with slotted spoon, reserving liquid. Coarsely chop shrimp, place in bowl, cover with SARAN WRAP and refrigerate. Add celery, onion and dill to reserved cooking liquid. Cover tightly with SARAN WRAP, turning back edge to vent. Microcook at 100% power 3 minutes.

Place mixture, covered, in refrigerator to thicken, about 30 minutes. Lightly oil 6-cup mold. Blend sour cream and mayonnaise until smooth. Stir into gelatin mixture. Add shrimp and parsley. Pour into prepared mold. Cover with SARAN WRAP and chill until set, about 4 hours. Unmold onto platter. Tuck lettuce around molded gelatin and serve with lemon wedges.

Conventional:　Sprinkle gelatin over 1 cup cold water in saucepan. Let stand 3 minutes to soften. Stir in lemon juice and salt. Heat to boiling. Add shrimp, cover and cook 3 minutes or until shrimp turn pink. Remove shrimp from cooking liquid with a slotted spoon, reserving liquid. Coarsely chop shrimp, place in bowl, cover with SARAN WRAP and refrigerate. Add celery, onion and dill to reserved cooking liquid. Cover and simmer 6 minutes. Chill, assemble and serve mousse as directed in microwave method.

Nice to know:　If you purchase shrimp that is already cleaned and cooked, you will need only 3/4 pound.

SHRIMPY FLOUNDER TURBANS

Microwave Cooking Time: 15 minutes　　　　　　　　*6 servings*
Conventional Cooking Time: 30 minutes

1 medium-size onion, chopped	1/4 pound cooked, cleaned shrimp, chopped
1 cup sliced mushrooms	2 tablespoons dry white wine (plus additional 1/2 cup in conventional method)
3 tablespoons butter or margarine	
1/2 teaspoon fines herbes	
1/2 teaspoon salt	6 flounder fillets (about 2 pounds)
1/4 teaspoon freshly ground pepper	
1 cup fresh bread cubes	Hollandaise Sauce (page 103)

Microwave:　　Butter six 6-ounce custard cups. Combine onion, mushrooms and butter in glass mixing bowl. Cover tightly with SARAN WRAP, turning back edge to vent. Microcook at 100% power 3 minutes. Stir in seasonings, bread cubes, shrimp and 2 tablespoons wine. Spoon a little stuffing onto darker side of each fillet. Roll up, starting at narrow end. Place one turban in each cup. Place cups in circle in microwave oven. Cover each cup tightly with SARAN WRAP, turning back edges to vent. Microcook at 70% power 12 to 14 minutes or until fish flakes easily, rotating cups once. Let stand 3 minutes. Invert turbans from cups and serve with Hollandaise Sauce.

Conventional:　　Butter 10 × 6-inch baking dish. Preheat oven to 350°. Sauté onion and mushrooms in butter until onion is transparent. Stir in seasonings, bread cubes, shrimp and 2 tablespoons wine. Spoon a little stuffing onto darker side of each fillet. Roll up, starting at narrow end. Place in prepared baking dish. Pour 1/2 cup wine around turbans and bake about 25 minutes or until fish flakes easily. Serve with Hollandaise Sauce.

Menu Hint:　　*Serve with steamed broccoli, parslied rice and garlic bread.*

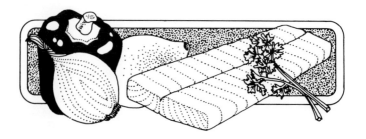

FISH IMPERIAL CASSEROLE

Microwave Cooking Time: 14 minutes   *4 servings*
Conventional Cooking Time: 32 minutes

1 onion, sliced
1 tablespoon lemon juice
2 sprigs parsley

1 bay leaf
   Salt and pepper to taste
1 pound cod fillets

Sauce:

1 egg, lightly beaten
2 tablespoons mayonnaise
1 tablespoon dry sherry
2 tablespoons dry mustard
   Salt and pepper to taste
1 green pepper, diced

2 tablespoons diced
   pimiento
2 tablespoons chopped
   parsley
   Paprika

Microwave: Place onion, lemon juice, parsley, bay leaf, salt, pepper and 1/2 cup water in 10 × 6-inch glass baking dish. Cover tightly with SARAN WRAP, turning back edge to vent. Microcook at 100% power 4 minutes. Add fish. Recover, leaving vent, and microcook at 100% power 5 minutes or until fish flakes easily. Let stand, covered, 3 minutes. Lift from cooking liquid with slotted spatula. Drain fish well and break into large flakes. Set aside. Lightly grease 1-quart casserole. Combine egg, mayonnaise, sherry, mustard, salt and pepper in medium-size bowl. Stir in green pepper, pimiento and parsley. Gently fold in flaked fish and spoon into prepared casserole. Sprinkle lightly with paprika. Cover tightly with SARAN WRAP, turning back edge to vent. Microcook at 70% power 5 minutes or until hot, rotating casserole once. Let stand, covered, 3 minutes.

Conventional: Place onion, lemon juice, parsley, bay leaf, salt, pepper and 1 cup water in 10-inch skillet. Heat to boiling. Reduce heat, cover and simmer 10 minutes. Add fish, cover and simmer 5 minutes or until fish flakes easily. Remove from cooking liquid with slotted spatula. Preheat oven to 375°. Assemble casserole as directed in microwave method. Bake 15 minutes or until heated through and top begins to brown.

POACHED SALMON

Microwave Cooking Time: 11 minutes   *4 servings*
Conventional Cooking Time: 17 minutes

1/2 cup dry white wine or dry vermouth	2 sprigs parsley
1 onion, sliced	4 salmon steaks, cut about
1 lemon, sliced	1/2-inch thick (about
1 1/2 teaspoons salt	2 pounds)
1/2 teaspoon peppercorns	Hollandaise Sauce
2 sprigs dill or 1/2 teaspoon dry dill	(page 103)

Microwave: Combine 1/2 cup water, wine, onion, lemon, salt, peppercorns, dill and parsley in 9-inch square glass baking dish. Cover tightly with SARAN WRAP, turning back edge to vent. Microcook at 100% power 3 minutes. Slip steaks into liquid, placing thickest parts at edge of dish. Recover, leaving vent, and microcook at 100% power 8 minutes or until fish is opaque and flakes easily when tested with fork. Rotate dish once during cooking. Let stand 3 minutes. Lift steaks from cooking liquid and place on serving platter. Pass Hollandaise Sauce at the table to spoon over steaks.

Conventional: Combine 2 cups water, wine, onion, lemon, salt, peppercorns, dill and parsley in large skillet. Heat to boiling. Reduce heat, cover and simmer 10 minutes. Add steaks, cover and simmer gently 5 minutes (or 10 minutes per inch), until fish flakes easily with fork. Lift steaks from cooking liquid and place on serving platter. Pass Hollandaise Sauce at the table to spoon over steaks.

Nice to know: Poached salmon steaks may also be served cold with Hollandaise Sauce, mayonnaise or lemon wedges.

SHRIMP CURRY

Microwave Cooking Time: 20 minutes   *4 servings*
Conventional Cooking Time: 22 minutes

1 1/2 pounds shrimp, peeled
    and cleaned
1 large onion, minced
2 cloves garlic, minced
2 tablespoons cooking oil
    (use 4 tablespoons in
    conventional method)
1 can (16 ounces) stewed
    tomatoes, coarsely
    chopped
2 tablespoons vinegar

2 teaspoons turmeric
2 teaspoons ginger
1 1/2 teaspoons salt
1 teaspoon cumin
1/4 teaspoon hot pepper
    sauce
1/2 cup dairy sour cream or
    plain yogurt
Chopped parsley for
    garnish
Hot cooked rice

Microwave: Place 1 1/2 cups water in 4-cup glass measure or casserole. Cover tightly with SARAN WRAP, turning back edge to vent. Microcook at 100% power 4 minutes or until boiling. Add shrimp. Recover, leaving vent, and microcook at 100% power 2 minutes. Let stand, covered, 3 minutes. Drain and set aside. Combine onion, garlic and oil in microsafe 2-quart cook-and-serve casserole. Cover tightly with SARAN WRAP, turning back edge to vent. Microcook at 100% power 3 minutes. Stir in undrained tomatoes, vinegar, turmeric, ginger, salt, cumin and hot pepper sauce. Recover, leaving vent, and microcook at 70% power 8 minutes or until slightly thickened, stirring once. Stir in drained shrimp and sour cream. Recover and microcook at 50% power 3 to 4 minutes or until hot. Garnish with parsley. Serve with rice.

Conventional: Heat 2 tablespoons oil in skillet. Add shrimp and sauté until shrimp are tender and pink, about 5 minutes. Remove shrimp from skillet and set aside. Add remaining 2 tablespoons oil, onion and garlic to skillet. Sauté until onion is transparent. Add undrained tomatoes, vinegar, turmeric, ginger, salt, cumin and hot pepper sauce. Simmer 10 minutes or until slightly thickened. Stir in sour cream and shrimp. Heat 2 to 3 minutes, stirring often. Garnish with parsley. Serve with rice.

MICROWAVE TIMING ADJUSTMENTS

The recipes in this book were developed and tested in a 625-watt variable-power microwave oven with 10 or more power settings. If your oven has a different wattage, fewer power settings, or if it is not a variable-power model, you will have to make adjustments in microwave cooking time.

The cooking times given for the recipes in this cookbook were correct and exact for the oven used on the day each recipe was tested. Nevertheless, every cook who uses this book must view the timing given as approximate. The reason for this is that microwave ovens often vary in wattage and in cooking patterns.

In addition, household current can affect the wattage of a microwave oven in the same way it can affect the temperature in a conventional electric oven. During peak load times, if there is another appliance on the same circuit or if your household voltage is normally low, the wattage in your microwave oven will be lower than it is rated. This means you will have to cook food somewhat longer than a recipe may recommend. On the other hand, you may be surprised to discover that occasionally food will cook somewhat faster than expected. Therefore, it is important to check food for doneness in a microwave oven in the same way you check it in a conventional oven — before you expect the food to be done.

When you round off cooking time in making conversions we suggest that you round it off on the low side, not the high, before you convert it. This will help you avoid overcooking food. You can always cook foods longer than you originally figured, but you can't undo the effects when you've cooked a dish too long. After you have made a time conversion for your oven, make a note on the recipe so you won't have to convert the time again the next time you prepare the same food.

Variable-Power Ovens

If the power settings on your microwave oven have names such as "high," "medium," or "medium-low" instead of percentage ratings, check your Use and Care Booklet to find out what the percentage of power is for each setting. If the settings do not draw exactly the same percentage of power as the power called for in a recipe, use the setting that is closest. For example, you may find that "medium-low" power on your oven is 45% power. Therefore you should use the "medium-low" setting when a recipe calls for 50% power; then add a few seconds or minutes to the cooking time, checking for doneness carefully and often.

VARIABLE-POWER OVEN TIME CONVERSIONS
(based on 5-minute intervals)

Wattage (at all power levels)

500W	6 min. 15 sec.
550W	5 min. 30 sec.
600W	5 min. 15 sec.
625W	5 min.
650W	4 min. 45 sec.
700W	4 min. 15 sec.

The times in this chart are equal to approximately 5 minutes of cooking time in a 625-watt microwave oven. To convert the microwave cooking time given on a recipe in this book to your oven, find the wattage of your oven in the chart and substitute the time shown for each 5 minutes of cooking time called for in our recipe.

Example 1: Our recipe calls for cooking at 50% power for 30 minutes: If you have a variable-power, 500-watt microwave oven, divide the 30 minutes by 5 to get the number of 5-minute intervals (6). Multiply the 6 intervals by 6 minutes, 15 seconds (37 minutes, 30 seconds). That means you should set your oven to microcook at 50% power for 37 minutes, 30 seconds.

Example 2: Our recipe calls for cooking at 70% power for 18 minutes: If you have a variable-power, 700-watt microwave oven, round the cooking time down from the 18 minutes to the nearest multiple of 5 (15 minutes). Then divide by 5 to get the number of 5-minute intervals (3). Multiply the 3 intervals by 4 minutes, 15 seconds (12 minutes, 45 seconds). That means you should set your oven to microcook at 70% power for 12 minutes, 45 seconds. Check for doneness and add additional cooking time if necessary.

Example 3: Our recipe calls for less than 5 minutes cooking time: If our recipe calls for 3 minutes microcooking, use about half the cooking time listed under the wattage for your oven. If the recipe calls for just 1 or 2 minutes of cooking time, microcook 1 or 2 minutes, check for doneness, then cook another 1 or 2 minutes if necessary.

Single-Power Ovens

If your microwave oven has a single power setting (high power), use this chart to convert our cooking times to your oven. Check your Use and Care Booklet to determine the wattage of your oven.

SINGLE-POWER OVEN TIME CONVERSIONS
(High Power)
(based on 5-minute intervals)

Wattage:	400	450	500
% power		Time	
100%	7 min. 45 sec.	6 min. 45 sec.	5 min. 30 sec.
90%	7 min.	6 min. 15 sec.	5 min. 30 sec.
70%	5 min. 15 sec.	4 min. 45 sec.	4 min. 15 sec.
50%	3 min. 45 sec.	3 min. 15 sec.	3 min.
30%	2 min. 15 sec.	2 min.	1 min. 45 sec.

The times in this chart are based on 5 minutes of microwave cooking in a 625-watt oven at various power levels. To convert the microwave cooking time given in a recipe in this book for your oven, find the wattage of your oven on the top line of the chart, then find the percentage of power called for in the recipe at the left-hand column of the chart. The time listed is the time base for your conversion cooking at high power. Substitute the number of minutes and seconds given for your oven, for each 5 minutes of cooking time called for in our recipe.

Example 1: Our recipe calls for cooking at 100% power for 5 minutes: If you have a 400-watt microwave oven, set your oven to microcook for 7 minutes, 45 seconds.

Example 2: Our recipe calls for cooking at 70% power for 10 minutes: If you have a 500-watt oven, divide the 10 minutes by 5 to get the number of 5 minute intervals (2). Multiply the 2 intervals by 4 minutes, 15 seconds (8 minutes, 30 seconds). Set your oven to microcook for 8 minutes, 30 seconds.

Example 3: Our recipe calls for cooking at 50% power for 28 minutes: If you have a 450-watt microwave oven, round the cooking time down from the 28 minutes to the nearest multiple of 5 (25 minutes). Then divide by 5 to get the number of 5-minute intervals (5). Multiply the 5 intervals by 3 minutes, 15 seconds (16 minutes, 15 seconds). That means you should set your oven to microcook for 16 minutes, 15 seconds. Check for doneness and add additional cooking time if necessary.

Example 4: Our recipe calls for less than 5 minutes cooking time: If our recipe calls for 3 minutes microcooking, use about half the cooking time listed under the wattage for your oven across from the appropriate percentage of power. If the recipe calls for just 1 or 2 minutes of cooking time, microcook 1 or 2 minutes, check for doneness, then cook for another 1 or 2 minutes if necessary.

Defrosting Hints and Tips

If you are using a variable-power oven, defrost food at 30% power, or follow the directions in the Use and Care Booklet provided with your oven.

When using a single-power oven, begin by checking the Conversion Chart for Single-Power Microwave Ovens on page 75. Use the time conversion given there with the Thawing Chart that follows to determine approximately how much time you will need to defrost a specific food. Divide the time into thirds. Microcook the frozen food for one-third of the total time suggested; let the food stand 5 minutes; microcook again for one-third of the total time; let stand 5 minutes; microcook again for the final one-third thawing time; let stand 10 minutes or the time recommended in the Thawing Chart, whichever is shorter. At this point the food should be thawed and be at refrigerator temperature. If it is not completely thawed, return it to the oven for a few minutes of additional defrosting.

Always transfer food from metal trays to microsafe dishes before defrosting, or, where appropriate, wrap in SARAN WRAP.

Remove metal twist-ties or metal tags from wrapped food. Be sure to remove the metal clamp found on most turkeys and on some frozen chickens.

Place the food on a rack in a shallow baking dish to catch liquid as the food defrosts.

Cover unwrapped food tightly with SARAN WRAP, turning back an edge to provide a vent.

Turn food over, or rotate food, at least once during thawing. Whenever possible, stir food or separate frozen pieces. If warm spots develop on a large piece of food like a roast, shield the warm areas with foil. If some pieces of food defrost more quickly than others, remove the defrosted pieces from the oven.

If water collects while food is defrosting, food that comes directly in contact with the water may begin to cook before the rest of the food has been defrosted. To avoid this problem, drain off any significant accumulation of water periodically.

Defrosted food should be refrigerator cold. Don't worry if a few ice crystals still remain on the food. They will melt during the final standing period.

You can save time by combining the defrosting and cooking capability of a microwave oven. Prepare food ahead of time, wrap it in SARAN WRAP or place it in a microsafe dish and cover it tightly with SARAN WRAP. Store it in the freezer. When you are ready to cook the food, take it from the freezer, turn back an edge of the SARAN WRAP to provide a vent, and place the food directly in the microwave oven to defrost. When the food is defrosted, proceed with microcooking. Remember, food that does not require a dish can be wrapped securely in SARAN WRAP, stored in the freezer and transferred, wrapped and vented, to your microwave oven for cooking.

Food that should not be cooked in a microwave oven should not be defrosted in a microwave oven either.

Thawing Chart

Times given below are approximate because the amount of time required to defrost food in a microwave oven is directly related to the size, shape and density of the food, as well as to the amount of food to be defrosted.

Food	Minutes per pound	Standing time after defrosting
Roast	10 to 12	15 to 25 min.
Ground meat		
1 pound	6 to 7	0
2 pounds	10 to 12	0
Cubed meat	6 to 8	5
Steaks	5 to 6	10
Chops and cutlets	4 to 6	10
Franks	3 to 5	0
Bacon	4 to 6	0
Link sausage	3 to 4	0
Bulk sausage	4 to 6	0
Chicken, whole	6 to 8	5
Chicken, cut up	5 to 6	0
Turkey, whole	10 to 12	15 to 20
Turkey parts	8 to 10	10
Cornish Hens	7 to 9	5
Duck	8 to 9	10
Whole fish	6 to 8	5
Fish fillets	8 to 10	5
Fish steaks	4 to 6	0
Shellfish	8 to 10	3
Vegetables (10 ounces)	5 to 7	4
Fruit (10 ounces)	5 to 7	4
Fruit pies (8 inch)	6 to 8	10
Cake	2 to 4	10
Bread and rolls	2 to 3	5

Converting Conventional Recipes

Some food cannot be cooked successfully in a microwave oven. Avoid recipes for crisp food, deep-fried food, chiffon and sponge cakes, most yeast breads and recipes for large quantities of food.

Whenever possible, use food that is shaped symmetrically. Round or square pieces of meat cook more evenly in a microwave oven than meat that is large at one end and tapers off at the other end, like a leg of lamb. Rolled, boneless cuts of meat and evenly cubed pieces of food are ideal.

You usually get best results if you microcook food in a round dish or oval dish. Where appropriate, a ring mold or a round dish with a glass placed in the center of the dish is the most satisfactory shape.

When there is liquid in a recipe it must be reduced by one-third to one-half. Microwave cooking is moist cooking; liquid is not reduced or evaporated by the cooking process.

Cooking time should be reduced to approximately one-third or one-half the time called for in the conventional method. Estimate time on the low side. You can always cook it a few minutes longer.

Most food should be covered during cooking. Exceptions are primarily bakery products. A cover keeps the moisture in the dish which, in turn, tenderizes the food and speeds cooking. A cover also serves to contain splatters. SARAN WRAP provides an ideal cover because it can be placed snugly over any shape dish and then vented to allow excess steam to escape.

Food must be stirred, rearranged, rotated or turned over in order to insure even cooking. This will prevent food from being overcooked at the edges and undercooked in the center. It will also prevent food from burning in one corner if your oven has a "hot spot."

Remember to allow for standing time after most dishes have been removed from the oven. In most cases, food should be covered with SARAN WRAP while standing. Cakes should be cooled in the cake dish on a heatproof surface, not on a rack.

Tests for doneness are very much the same for microcooked food as they are for conventionally cooked food. However, food may not "look" the same because food cooked in a microwave oven tends to be light in color. A cake is done even when the center of the top still looks moist. If you touch the moist spot, you will discover a fully baked cake just under the moist surface.

Varied & Versatile

CURRIED VEGETABLES

Microwave Cooking Time: 17 minutes
Conventional Cooking Time: 22 minutes

6 to 8 servings

1/4 cup butter or margarine
1 large onion, cut into thin wedges
1 clove garlic, minced
2 teaspoons curry
1 teaspoon salt
1/4 teaspoon freshly ground pepper

4 cups cauliflowerettes (about 1/2 medium-size head)
1 green pepper, cut into strips
2 stalks celery, sliced
3 carrots, sliced
1 pound zucchini, cut into thin strips

Microwave: Combine butter, onion, garlic, curry, salt and pepper in 3-quart casserole. Microcook at 100% power 4 minutes, stirring once. Stir in cauliflower, green pepper, celery, carrots and 2/3 cup water. Cover tightly with SARAN WRAP, turning back edge to vent. Microcook at 100% power 10 minutes, stirring once. Fold in zucchini, recover, leaving vent, and microcook at 100% power 3 minutes or until just tender, stirring twice.

Conventional: Sauté onion, garlic and butter in large skillet until transparent. Stir in curry, salt and pepper and cook 2 minutes longer. Add cauliflower, green pepper, celery, carrots and 1 cup water. Heat to boiling. Reduce heat, cover and simmer 10 minutes. Stir in zucchini, cover and simmer 5 minutes or until just tender.

Menu Hint: Serve this rather special, spicy vegetable dish as a colorful accompaniment to baked chicken, broiled lamb or fish. A spoonful of cooking liquid is delicious spooned over parslied rice.

TANGY CELERY

Microwave Cooking Time: 16 minutes   *4 servings*
Conventional Cooking Time: 22 minutes

1/4 cup white wine vinegar	1 large bunch celery or
1 teaspoon dill	2 celery hearts
1 teaspoon sugar	Thinly sliced pimiento or
1/2 teaspoon salt	red pepper for garnish
1/8 teaspoon pepper	

Microwave: Stir vinegar, dill, sugar, salt, pepper and 3/4 cup water in 12 × 8-inch glass baking dish. Microcook at 100% power 5 minutes. Stir well.

Meanwhile, cut off leafy top portion of celery. Pull off tough outer ribs and save to use another time. Cut remaining celery stalks lengthwise into 4 strips or cut celery hearts lengthwise in half. Layer in liquid in baking dish, alternating tops and bottoms at each end of dish. Cover tightly with SARAN WRAP, turning back edge to vent. Microcook at 100% power 11 minutes or until celery is fork-tender, rotating dish once. Chill in liquid. To serve, remove from cooking liquid and sprinkle with sliced pimiento.

Conventional: Combine vinegar, dill, sugar, salt, pepper and 1 1/2 cups water in 10-inch skillet. Heat to boiling. Cover and simmer 5 minutes. Meanwhile, cut celery as directed in microwave method. Add to simmering liquid. Cover and simmer 15 minutes or until fork-tender. Chill in liquid. To serve, remove from cooking liquid and sprinkle with sliced pimiento.

Variation: Place on lettuce and top each serving with 1 tablespoon olive oil. This vegetable may also be served hot.

SPRING VEGETABLES

Microwave Cooking Time: 16 minutes   *6 servings*
Conventional Cooking Time: 27 minutes

1/2 pound tiny white onions,
       peeled
2 tablespoons butter or
       margarine
1 pound small new
       potatoes, scrubbed
6 carrots, peeled and cut
       into 1-inch pieces

1/2 cup chicken broth
2 tablespoons chopped
       fresh dill or 1 teaspoon
       dried dill
3/4 teaspoon salt
1 cup peas (preferably
       fresh)

Microwave: Combine onions and butter in 2-quart glass bowl or casserole. Cover tightly with SARAN WRAP, turning back edge to vent. Microcook at 100% power 3 minutes. Add potatoes, carrots, chicken broth, dill and salt. Recover, leaving vent, and microcook at 100% power 10 minutes, stirring once. Add peas, recover and microcook at 100% power 3 minutes longer or until vegetables are just tender.

Conventional: Sauté onions in butter until slightly browned, about 5 minutes. Add potatoes, carrots, chicken broth, dill and salt. Heat to boiling. Reduce heat, cover and simmer 15 minutes. Add peas, recover and cook 5 minutes longer or until vegetables are just tender.

Nice to know: Cut ends off unpeeled onions. Place in small casserole. Cover tightly with SARAN WRAP, turning back edge to vent. Microcook at 100% power 1 1/2 minutes. Let stand a few minutes, then remove skins without tears.

GREEN BEANS AND ZUCCHINI

Microwave Cooking Time: 21 minutes   *6 servings*
Conventional Cooking Time: 30 minutes

4 slices bacon, diced
1 onion, diced
1 pound fresh green beans,
       cut into 1-inch pieces

1 teaspoon salt
1/4 teaspoon pepper
1/2 pound zucchini, sliced

Microwave: Combine bacon and onion in 2-quart casserole. Cover tightly with SARAN WRAP, turning back edge to vent. Microcook at 100% power 5 minutes or until bacon is lightly browned. Add beans, salt, pepper and 2/3 cup water. Recover, leaving vent, and microcook at 100% power 13 minutes, stirring once. Add zucchini, stir well, recover and microcook 3 minutes longer. Stir and serve immediately.

Conventional: Sauté bacon and onion in large saucepan until onion is transparent and bacon is lightly browned. Add beans, salt, pepper and 1 cup water. Heat to boiling. Reduce heat, cover and simmer 20 minutes. Add zucchini, stir well, cover and simmer 5 minutes. Stir and serve immediately.

STUFFED MUSHROOM CAPS

Microwave Cooking Time: 10 minutes   *6 servings*
Conventional Cooking Time: 20 minutes

12 large mushrooms (each about 2 inches in diameter)
3 tablespoons chopped onion
2 tablespoons chopped green pepper
3 tablespoons butter or margarine, divided
1/2 cup fresh bread crumbs (about 1 slice)
1 tablespoon chopped parsley
1/4 teaspoon salt
1/8 teaspoon freshly ground pepper
1/8 teaspoon thyme

Microwave: Wipe mushrooms with damp cloth. Trim and discard thin slice from bottom of each stem. Gently pull stems from caps and mince. Combine minced stems, onion, green pepper and 1 tablespoon butter in 2-cup glass measure. Cover tightly with SARAN WRAP, turning back edge to vent. Microcook at 100% power 3 minutes. Stir in bread crumbs, parsley, salt, pepper and thyme, and set aside. Place remaining 2 tablespoons butter in 8-inch round glass baking dish. Microcook at 100% power 1 minute. Brush mushroom caps with melted butter. Spoon stuffing mixture into caps and place in circle in baking dish, stuffing side up. Cover tightly with SARAN WRAP, turning back edge to vent. Microcook at 100% 6 minutes or until mushrooms are tender.

Conventional: Preheat oven to 350°. Wipe mushrooms with damp cloth and mince stems as directed in microwave method. Melt 2 tablespoons butter in skillet. Sauté minced mushroom stems, onion and green pepper until onion is transparent. Remove from heat. Stir in bread crumbs, parsley, salt, pepper and thyme, and set aside. Melt remaining 1 tablespoon butter; brush mushroom caps with melted butter. Spoon stuffing into caps and place in baking dish, stuffing side up. Bake 15 minutes or until stuffing is lightly browned.

RATATOUILLE

Microwave Cooking Time: 26 minutes　　　　　　　　　*6 to 8 servings*
Conventional Cooking Time: 40 minutes

2 medium-size onions, coarsely chopped	1 pound zucchini, cut into chunks
2 green peppers, chopped	1 pound eggplant, peeled and cut into chunks
2 cloves garlic, minced	1 pound tomatoes, cut into chunks
1/4 cup olive oil	
1 1/2 teaspoons basil	1/2 cup chopped parsley
1 1/4 teaspoons salt	
1/4 teaspoon pepper	

Microwave:　Combine onion, green pepper, garlic and olive oil in 4-quart glass bowl. Cover tightly with SARAN WRAP, turning back edge to vent. Microcook at 100% power 6 minutes, stirring once. Sprinkle with seasonings. Stir in zucchini, eggplant and tomatoes. Recover, leaving vent, and microcook at 100% power 8 minutes, then at 70% power 12 minutes, stirring once during each cooking stage. Fold in parsley. Serve warm or chilled.

Conventional:　Sauté onions, green peppers and garlic in olive oil until onion is transparent, about 10 minutes. Add zucchini and eggplant and sauté 5 minutes longer. Stir in tomatoes and seasonings. Reduce heat, cover and simmer 25 minutes, stirring occasionally; fold in parsley. Serve warm or chilled.

Menu Hint:　This well-seasoned dish is delicious hot or cold, with baked chicken, tossed salad and crusty French bread.

DILLED CARROTS

Microwave Cooking Time: 6 minutes　　　　　　　　　*4 to 6 servings*
Conventional Cooking Time: 8 minutes

1 pound carrots, sliced or cut into julienne strips	1 teaspoon dill
2 tablespoons butter or margarine	1/2 teaspoon salt
	Dash freshly ground pepper

Microwave:　Combine carrots, butter, dill, salt, pepper and 1 tablespoon water in 1 1/2-quart glass bowl. Cover tightly with SARAN WRAP, turning back edge to vent. Microcook at 100% power 6 minutes, stirring once. Let stand, covered, 2 minutes. Stir and spoon into serving dish.

Conventional: Place carrots and 1/4 cup water in 2-quart saucepan. Heat to boiling. Reduce heat, cover, and simmer 8 minutes or until tender. Drain. Add butter, dill, salt and pepper. Let stand until butter melts. Stir lightly and spoon into serving dish.

SOUFFLE-STYLE SPINACH

Microwave Cooking Time: 23 minutes   *6 servings*
Conventional Cooking Time: 51 minutes

1 small onion, minced	3/4 cup dairy sour cream
2 tablespoons butter or margarine	2 eggs, well beaten
	1 tablespoon lemon juice
2 packages (10 ounces each) fresh spinach	3/4 teaspoon salt
	Dash nutmeg

Microwave: Grease 5- to 6-cup soufflé dish or casserole. Combine onion and butter in 4-quart casserole. Cover tightly with SARAN WRAP, turning back edge to vent. Microcook at 100% power 3 minutes. Rinse spinach, removing stems and tough ribs. Drain well and place in casserole. Recover, leaving vent, and microcook at 100% power 6 minutes, stirring at least once.

Drain spinach, discarding cooking liquid. Finely chop with large knife or in food processor. Combine sour cream, eggs, lemon juice, salt and nutmeg. Add spinach and mix well. Pour into soufflé dish. Cover tightly with SARAN WRAP, turning back edge to vent. Microcook at 50% power 7 minutes. Stir cooked edge to center. Recover, leaving vent, and microcook at 50% power 7 minutes longer or until set. Let stand 5 minutes before serving.

Conventional: Grease 5- to 6-cup soufflé dish or casserole. Preheat oven to 350°. In Dutch oven sauté onion and butter until onion is transparent. Rinse spinach, removing stems and tough ribs. Drain well and place in Dutch oven. Cover and cook until spinach wilts, 6 to 8 minutes. Drain spinach, chop and assemble casserole as directed in microwave method. Pour into soufflé dish. Place on rack in large baking dish and add boiling water to come halfway up side of dish. Bake 35 to 40 minutes or until knife inserted in center comes out clean. Remove from water bath and let stand 5 minutes before serving.

Nice to know: This dish will not rise like a soufflé nor will it fall when removed from the oven.

SPAGHETTI SQUASH

Microwave Cooking Time: 14 minutes   *4 to 6 servings*
Conventional Cooking Time: 42 minutes

1 **3-pound spaghetti squash**	1/4 **cup chopped parsley,**
1/4 **cup butter or margarine**	1/4 **cup grated Parmesan**
1 **clove garlic, minced**	**cheese or 1/4 cup dairy**
3/4 **teaspoon salt**	**sour cream**
Freshly ground pepper to taste	

Microwave: Pierce squash 3 or 4 times with thin knife. Wrap in SARAN WRAP, leaving seam for vent. Set wrapped squash on microsafe plate or pie plate. Microcook at 100% power 12 or 13 minutes or until squash is fork-tender, turning squash over and rotating twice. Let stand 5 minutes. Place butter and garlic in 1-cup glass measure. Microcook at 100% power 2 minutes. Stir in salt. Cut squash lengthwise in half. Scoop out and discard seeds and stringy portion in center. With fork, fluff solid portion of squash into spaghetti-like strands. Combine "spaghetti" strands with butter and chopped parsley, Parmesan cheese or sour cream.

Conventional: Cook whole spaghetti squash in simmering water to cover 35 to 40 minutes or until fork-tender. Remove from water and let stand 5 minutes. Meanwhile, melt butter with garlic in small saucepan. Simmer 1 to 2 minutes to release garlic flavor. Add salt. Cut squash in half and serve as directed in microwave method.

ASPARAGUS VINAIGRETTE

Microwave Cooking Time: 6 minutes   *4 servings*
Conventional Cooking Time: 9 minutes

1 **pound fresh asparagus**	1 **teaspoon sugar**
1/4 **cup dry white wine or cider vinegar**	1/2 **teaspoon dry mustard**
1 **tablespoon grated onion**	1/2 **teaspoon salt**
2 **teaspoons grated lemon peel**	**Dairy sour cream (optional)**

Microwave: Wash asparagus. Break off and discard tough bottom part of stalks. Place asparagus in 8 × 4-inch glass loaf pan, arranging stalks to face in alternate directions. Mix 1/4 cup water, vinegar, onion, lemon peel, sugar, mustard and salt. Pour over asparagus. Cover tightly with SARAN WRAP, turning back edge to vent. Microcook at 100% power 3 minutes. Stir asparagus gently, moving stalks from middle of dish to outside of dish. Recover, leaving vent, and microcook at 100% power 3 to 4 minutes longer or until tender-crisp. Let stand 3 minutes. Serve with small dollop of sour cream, if desired.

Conventional: Wash asparagus. Break off and discard tough bottom part of stalks. Place asparagus in 9-inch skillet. Mix 1/2 cup water, vinegar, onion, lemon peel, sugar, mustard and salt. Pour over asparagus. Cover and heat to boiling. Reduce heat and simmer 7 to 8 minutes or until tender-crisp. Serve with small dollop of sour cream, if desired.

TOMATO-ZUCCHINI CASSEROLE

Microwave Cooking Time: 9 1/2 minutes   *4 to 6 servings*
Conventional Cooking Time: 26 minutes

3 tablespoons butter or margarine, divided	1/2 teaspoon oregano
3 small zucchini (about 1 pound), sliced	1/2 teaspoon salt
3/4 cup fresh bread crumbs	Dash freshly ground pepper
1/4 cup grated Parmesan cheese	2 medium-size tomatoes, sliced
2 tablespoons chopped parsley	

Microwave: Place 1 1/2 tablespoons butter in 8-inch round glass baking dish. Microcook at 100% power 1 1/2 minutes. Tilt dish to spread butter evenly.
Layer half the zucchini slices in butter. Mix bread crumbs, Parmesan cheese, parsley, oregano, salt and pepper. Sprinkle 1/3 cup bread crumb mixture over zucchini. Top with tomato slices; add another layer of bread crumbs; layer remaining zucchini on top; sprinkle with bread crumbs; dot with butter. Cover tightly with SARAN WRAP, turning back edge to vent. Microcook at 100% power 8 minutes, rotating dish once. Let stand 5 minutes.

Conventional: Preheat oven to 350°. Melt butter in small saucepan. Pour half the butter into 8-inch baking dish or casserole. Layer zucchini, tomatoes and bread crumb mixture as directed in microwave method. Drizzle with remaining melted butter. Bake 20 to 25 minutes or until zucchini is fork-tender.

SOY

MICROWAVE
cooking
FREEZING

MICROWAVE
Cooking
& FREEZING

STIR-FRIED BROCCOLI AND CAULIFLOWER

Microwave Cooking Time: 7 minutes　　　　　　　　*4 servings*
Conventional Cooking Time: 10 minutes

1/2 **bunch broccoli**	1 **tablespoon sesame seed**
1/2 **medium-size head**	2 **tablespoons soy sauce**
cauliflower	1/4 **teaspoon ginger**
3 **tablespoons cooking oil**	1/4 **teaspoon salt**

Microwave: Cut broccoli and cauliflower into small flowerettes about 1-inch long and 1/2-inch thick. Heat 10-inch square browning dish at 100% power 3 minutes. Add oil and tilt dish (using pot holder) to coat evenly. Add broccoli and cauliflower. Stir well to coat with oil. Cover with glass lid and microcook at 100% power 4 to 5 minutes, stirring once. Sprinkle with sesame seed. Mix soy sauce, ginger and salt. Pour over vegetables and toss to coat. Serve immediately.

Conventional: Cut broccoli and cauliflower into small flowerettes about 1-inch long and 1/2-inch thick. Heat oil over high heat in skillet or Dutch oven. Add broccoli and cauliflower. Stir quickly to coat with oil. Reduce heat slightly, add 3 tablespoons water, cover and steam 3 minutes. Uncover and stir-fry 3 to 5 minutes longer. Sprinkle with sesame seed. Mix soy sauce, ginger and salt. Pour over vegetables and toss to coat. Serve immediately.

CREAMY WILTED ESCAROLE

Microwave Cooking Time: 7 minutes   *4 servings*
Conventional Cooking Time: 10 minutes

3 slices bacon, diced	Dash freshly ground
2 tablespoons chopped	pepper
onion	1 bunch escarole (about 1
1/4 cup red wine vinegar	pound), washed and cut
2 tablespoons sugar	into bite-size pieces
2 teaspoons dry mustard	1/4 cup dairy sour cream
1/2 teaspoon salt	

Microwave: Combine bacon and onion in 3-quart glass bowl. Cover tightly with SARAN WRAP, turning back edge to vent. Microcook at 100% power 5 minutes or until bacon is lightly browned. Stir in vinegar, sugar, mustard, salt and pepper. Add escarole and toss well. Recover, leaving vent, and microcook at 100% power 2 minutes, or until escarole wilts. Add sour cream, toss well and serve immediately.

Conventional: Sauté bacon and onion in large skillet until onion is transparent and bacon is browned. Stir in vinegar, sugar, mustard, salt and pepper. Heat to simmering. Add escarole, cover and cook 2 to 3 minutes or until escarole wilts. Add sour cream, toss well and serve immediately.

BRANDIED MUSHROOMS

Microwave Cooking Time: 8 minutes   *4 servings*
Conventional Cooking Time: 15 minutes

1 package (12 ounces)	1/8 teaspoon freshly ground
small mushrooms, sliced	pepper
1 onion, minced	1 tablespoon all-purpose
2 tablespoons butter or	flour
margarine (use 3 table-	1/2 cup dry vermouth
spoons in conventional	1 tablespoon brandy
method)	2 tablespoons chopped
1/4 teaspoon salt	parsley

Microwave: Place mushrooms, onion, butter, salt and pepper in 2-quart glass bowl or casserole. Cover tightly with SARAN WRAP, turning back edge to vent. Microcook at 100% power 5 minutes, stirring once. Blend flour and vermouth until smooth, stir into mushrooms. Recover, leaving vent, and microcook at 100% power 3 minutes, stirring twice. Stir in brandy and parsley. Season to taste and serve immediately.

Conventional: Sauté mushrooms and onion in 3 table-spoons butter until all liquid is absorbed, about 10 minutes. Add flour, salt and pepper and stir until smooth. Blend in vermouth and 2 tablespoons water. Cook, stirring constantly until thickened. Add brandy and parsley. Season to taste and serve immediately.

HONEY-ORANGE SQUASH

Microwave Cooking Time: 14 minutes　　　　　　　　　*4 servings*
Conventional Cooking Time: 1 hour, 7 minutes

2/3　cup honey or maple 　　　syrup	1　tablespoon grated 　　　orange peel
1/4　cup butter or margarine	2　acorn squash
1/2　teaspoon salt	

Microwave: Combine honey, butter, salt and orange peel in 2-cup glass measure. Cover tightly with SARAN WRAP, turning back edge to vent. Microcook at 100% power 4 to 5 minutes or until butter melts. Set aside. Cut squash in half lengthwise and scoop out seeds. Trim off thin slice from rounded sides so squash halves will sit firmly, cut side up. Arrange squash, cut side down, in glass baking dish. Cover tightly with SARAN WRAP, turning back edge to vent. Microcook at 100% power 5 minutes. Turn cut side up. Divide honey mixture in squash halves and brush cut surfaces of squash with a little honey mixture. Recover, leaving vent, and microcook at 100% power 5 to 6 minutes or until fork-tender, rotating dish once during cooking. Let stand, covered, 5 minutes.

Conventional: Preheat oven to 350°. Cut squash in half lengthwise and scoop out seeds. Trim off thin slice from rounded sides so squash halves will sit firmly, cut side up. Place squash, cut side down, in large baking dish. Add 1/2 cup water and bake 30 minutes. Melt butter in small saucepan. Stir in honey, salt and orange peel. Turn squash halves cut side up. Divide honey mixture in squash halves and brush cut surfaces of squash with a little honey mixture. Bake 25 to 30 minutes longer or until fork-tender.

Variation:　Omit honey mixture. Microcook or bake squash as above. Brush cut surfaces with melted butter when squash is turned cut side up. Prepare 1 package (10 ounces) frozen peas according to package directions or in microwave oven. Drain, add 2 tablespoons butter or margarine, 1/2 teaspoon dill or mint and 1/2 teaspoon salt. Toss until butter melts. Spoon into squash halves and serve immediately.

GERMAN RED CABBAGE

Microwave Cooking Time: 17 minutes   *6 servings*
Conventional Cooking Time: 25 minutes

1 **head red cabbage (about 1 pound), shredded (about 5 cups)**	1 **teaspoon salt**
1 **onion, sliced**	1/4 **teaspoon freshly ground pepper**
1 **apple, cored and diced**	1/4 **teaspoon allspice**
1/2 **cup cider vinegar**	1/4 **teaspoon cloves**
1/2 **cup apple juice or water (use 1 cup in conventional method)**	1/4 **cup sugar**
	1 **tablespoon cornstarch**

Microwave: Combine cabbage, onion, apple, vinegar, apple juice, salt, pepper, allspice and cloves in 3-quart casserole. Cover tightly with SARAN WRAP, turning back edge to vent. Micro-cook at 100% power 15 minutes, stirring once. Mix sugar and cornstarch. Stir into cabbage mixture. Recover, leaving vent, and microcook at 100% power 2 minutes or until mixture boils and sauce is clear. Serve immediately.

Conventional: Mix cabbage, onion, apple, vinegar, 1 cup apple juice, salt, pepper, allspice and cloves in large saucepan. Heat to boiling. Reduce heat, cover and simmer 20 minutes. Mix sugar and cornstarch. Stir into cabbage mixture. Heat to boiling, stirring constantly. Boil 1 minute. Serve immediately.

CORN PUDDING

Microwave Cooking Time: 23 minutes   *6 to 8 servings*
Conventional Cooking Time: 55 minutes

6 **slices bacon, diced, or 1/2 cup diced ham**	3/4 **teaspoon salt**
1 **onion, diced**	1/4 **teaspoon pepper**
1/2 **cup diced green pepper**	3 **eggs, well beaten**
1 2/3 **cups milk**	
1 **package (10 ounces) frozen whole-kernel corn**	

Microwave: Combine bacon, onion and green pepper in 1 1/2-quart casserole. Cover tightly with SARAN WRAP, turning back edge to vent. Microcook at 100% power 5 minutes, stirring once. Add milk, corn, salt and pepper. Recover, leaving vent, and microcook at 100% power 5 to 6 minutes or until steaming. Beat a little hot mixture into eggs. Pour eggs back into casserole, stirring. Recover and microcook at 50% power 13 to 14 minutes or until custard is set, stirring cooked part toward center after 6 minutes and rotating casserole twice. Let stand, covered, 10 minutes before serving.

Conventional: Butter 1 1/2-quart casserole. Preheat oven to 350°. Sauté bacon, onion and green pepper in skillet until onion is transparent. Spoon into casserole. Add milk, corn, salt, pepper and eggs. Stir until well mixed. Bake 50 minutes or until knife inserted in center of custard comes out clean. Let stand 5 minutes before serving.

HOT BROCCOLI VINAIGRETTE

Microwave Cooking Time: 9 minutes   *4 to 6 servings*
Conventional Cooking Time: 14 minutes

1 **bunch broccoli (about**	3 **tablespoons olive oil**
1 1/2 pounds)	2 **teaspoons dry mustard**
4 **tablespoons cider**	2 **teaspoons sugar**
vinegar, divided	3/4 **teaspoon salt**

Microwave: Wash broccoli. Cut off and discard all but 4 inches of broccoli spears. Divide into 1/2-inch thick spears. Arrange in 2 rows in 12 × 8-inch glass baking dish, placing flowerettes in center of dish. Add 1/3 cup water and 2 tablespoons vinegar. Cover tightly with SARAN WRAP, turning back edge to vent. Microcook at 100% power 8 to 10 minutes or until crisp but tender, rotating dish once. Combine remaining 2 tablespoons vinegar, olive oil, mustard, sugar and salt in 2-cup glass measure. Microcook at 100% power 1 minute or until hot. Lift broccoli from cooking liquid and place on serving platter. Pour oil mixture over and serve immediately.

Conventional: Wash and cut broccoli as directed in microwave method. Layer spears in skillet; add 1/2 cup water and 2 tablespoons vinegar. Cover and bring to a boil, reduce heat and simmer 10 minutes. In small saucepan, heat remaining 2 tablespoons vinegar, olive oil, mustard, sugar and salt. Lift broccoli from cooking liquid and place on serving platter. Pour oil mixture over and serve immediately.

Nice to know: Hot Broccoli Vinaigrette can be served as an unusual alternative to a tossed salad. Its crispy, crunchy texture is delightful hot or cold. For added interest, sprinkle with chopped, hard-cooked egg.

TOMATO ASPIC

Microwave Cooking Time: 7 minutes   *6 to 8 servings*
Conventional Cooking Time: 12 minutes

2 envelopes unflavored
   gelatin
2 cups tomato juice
1 can (6 ounces) tomato
   paste
1 small onion, minced
1/2 small green pepper,
   finely diced
1 stalk celery, finely
   chopped

3 tablespoons lemon juice
2 tablespoons cider
   vinegar
3/4 teaspoon salt
1/2 teaspoon oregano
   Lettuce leaves
   Lemon wedges

Microwave: Sprinkle gelatin over tomato juice in 2-quart glass bowl or casserole. Let stand 3 minutes. Stir in tomato paste, onion, green pepper, celery, lemon juice, vinegar, salt and oregano. Cover tightly with SARAN WRAP, turning back edge to vent. Microcook at 100% power 7 minutes, stirring once. Pour into 4- to 5-cup glass mold or bowl. Cover with SARAN WRAP and chill until set, about 4 hours. To serve, cover with serving dish, invert and unmold. Tuck lettuce leaves around mold and serve with lemon wedges.

Conventional: Sprinkle gelatin over tomato juice in saucepan. Let stand 3 minutes. Stir in tomato paste, onion, green pepper, celery, lemon juice, vinegar, salt and oregano. Heat to simmering. Simmer 10 minutes, stirring frequently. Pour into 4- to 5-cup mold or bowl and chill until set, about 4 hours. To serve, cover with serving dish, invert and unmold. Tuck lettuce leaves around mold and serve with lemon wedges.

Tomato Aspic, Hot Broccoli Vinaigrette (page 93)

MEXICAN PEPPER SALAD

Microwave Cooking Time: 7 minutes   *6 servings*
Conventional Cooking Time: 15 minutes

2 large green peppers	1/2 teaspoon salt
1/3 cup salad oil	2 tomatoes, cut into chunks
1/4 cup red wine vinegar	1 small cucumber, diced
1 clove garlic, minced	2 scallions, sliced
1/2 teaspoon oregano	Lettuce leaves

Microwave: Rinse peppers and dry thoroughly. Wrap each pepper in SARAN WRAP, leaving seam for vent. Place on microsafe plate and microcook at 100% power 7 to 8 minutes, turning peppers over once. Let stand, wrapped, 10 to 15 minutes until skin wrinkles and pulls off easily.

Rub skin off under cold running water. Halve peppers, remove seeds and membranes and cut into 1-inch squares. Combine oil, vinegar, garlic, oregano and salt in bowl. Add peppers. Cover tightly with SARAN WRAP and marinate 2 to 3 hours or overnight. Add tomatoes, cucumber and scallions and toss lightly. Serve on lettuce leaves.

Conventional: Preheat broiler. Place washed peppers on broiler pan. Broil about 15 minutes close to heat, until charred, turning peppers often. Wrap hot peppers in SARAN WRAP and let stand 10 to 15 minutes or until skin wrinkles and pulls off easily. Rub off skin, marinate peppers and prepare salad as directed in microwave method.

CINNAMON-APPLE SWEET POTATOES

Microwave Cooking Time: 18 minutes   *6 servings*
Conventional Cooking Time: 45 minutes

1 pound sweet potatoes (2 medium-size), peeled	1 tablespoon lemon juice
3 small apples, cored and sliced	3/4 teaspoon salt
3/4 cup orange juice	1/2 teaspoon cinnamon
1/4 cup firmly packed brown sugar	1 tablespoon butter or margarine
	1/3 cup chopped pecans

Microwave: Grease 1 1/2-quart casserole. Slice sweet potatoes and layer alternately with apples in prepared casserole. Mix orange juice, brown sugar, lemon juice, salt and cinnamon. Pour over potatoes and apples. Dot with butter and sprinkle with nuts. Cover tightly with SARAN WRAP, turning back edge to vent. Microcook at 100% power 18 minutes or until potatoes are fork-tender, spooning sauce over and rotating casserole twice. Let stand, covered, 5 minutes before serving.

Conventional: Grease 1 1/2-quart casserole. Preheat oven to 350°. Slice sweet potatoes and assemble casserole as directed in microwave method. Bake 40 to 45 minutes or until potatoes are fork-tender, basting with sauce once or twice during cooking.

Nice to know: If your brown sugar hardens, place in box in microwave oven and microcook at 50% power about 2 minutes.

HOT POTATO-APPLE SALAD

Microwave Cooking Time: 12 minutes   *8 servings*
Conventional Cooking Time: 15 minutes

4	slices bacon, diced	1/2	teaspoon caraway seed
1	onion, coarsely chopped		(optional)
1	stalk celery, chopped	4	medium-size potatoes,
1/4	cup cider vinegar		cubed and cooked
2	tablespoons sugar		(about 4 cups)
1 1/2	teaspoons salt	2	apples, cored and diced
1/4	teaspoon pepper	1/4	cup chopped parsley

Microwave: Combine bacon, onion and celery in large glass bowl. Cover tightly with SARAN WRAP, turning back edge to vent. Microcook at 100% power 5 minutes. Stir in vinegar, sugar, salt, pepper and caraway seed. Recover, leaving vent, and microcook at 100% power 2 minutes. Add potatoes, recover and microcook at 70% power 5 minutes or until potatoes are hot. Stir once. Add apples and parsley and toss gently. Serve immediately.

Conventional: Sauté bacon, onion and celery in large skillet until onion is transparent, about 5 minutes. Stir in vinegar, sugar, salt, pepper and caraway seed. Heat. Add potatoes, cover and cook until potatoes are just hot. Gently stir in apples and parsley and serve immediately.

Nice to know: To cook potatoes in microwave oven, peel, cut into 1/2-inch cubes and place in large glass bowl. Add 1 cup water. Cover tightly with SARAN WRAP, turning back edge to vent. Microcook at 100% power 10 minutes. Let stand, covered, 5 minutes. Drain well.

BANANA-YAM CASSEROLE

Microwave Cooking Time: 10 minutes   *6 servings*
Conventional Cooking Time: 25 minutes

1 **can (18 ounces) sweet potatoes or yams**	1/8 **teaspoon nutmeg or cinnamon**
3 **medium-size bananas**	1/4 **cup firmly packed brown sugar**
1/3 **cup orange juice**	1 **tablespoon butter or margarine**
2 **tablespoons lemon juice**	
1/2 **teaspoon salt**	

Microwave: Lightly grease 1 1/2-quart casserole. Slice sweet potatoes and bananas and place in casserole. Mix orange juice, lemon juice, salt and nutmeg. Pour over sweet potatoes and toss well to coat. Sprinkle brown sugar over top and dot with butter. Cover tightly with SARAN WRAP, turning back edge to vent. Microcook at 70% power 10 minutes, rotating dish twice. Let stand, covered, 5 minutes.

Conventional: Preheat oven to 350°. Lightly grease 1 1/2-quart casserole. Slice sweet potatoes and bananas and place in prepared casserole. Mix orange juice, lemon juice, salt and nutmeg. Pour over sweet potatoes and toss well to coat. Sprinkle brown sugar over top and dot with butter. Bake, uncovered, 20 to 25 minutes.

SCALLOPED POTATOES

Microwave Cooking Time: 31 minutes   *6 servings*
Conventional Cooking Time: 1 hour, 10 minutes

3 **tablespoons butter or margarine**	1 3/4 **cups milk (use 2 cups in conventional method)**
2 **tablespoons all-purpose flour**	4 **medium-size potatoes, peeled and thinly sliced (about 4 cups)**
1 1/2 **teaspoons salt**	
1/2 **teaspoon pepper**	1 **large onion, thinly sliced**
1/2 **teaspoon paprika**	

Microwave: Grease 2-quart microsafe ring mold. Place butter in 4-cup glass measure. Microcook at 100% power 1 minute. Stir in flour, salt, pepper and paprika until smooth. Blend in milk. Cover tightly with SARAN WRAP, turning back edge to vent. Microcook at 100% power 5 minutes, until thickened, stirring twice. Layer potatoes and onion slices alternately in prepared mold, starting and ending with potatoes. Pour sauce over potatoes and sprinkle with paprika. Cover dish tightly with

SARAN WRAP, turning back edge to vent. Microcook at 50% power about 25 minutes or until potatoes are fork-tender, rotating dish twice. Let stand on heatproof surface 5 minutes before serving.

Conventional: Grease 2-quart casserole. Preheat oven to 375°. Melt butter in saucepan. Stir in flour, salt, pepper and paprika until smooth. Gradually stir in 2 cups milk. Cook, stirring constantly, until thickened, about 5 minutes. Layer potatoes and onion slices alternately in prepared casserole, starting and ending with potatoes. Pour sauce over potatoes and sprinkle with paprika. Cover and bake 45 minutes. Uncover and bake 15 minutes longer or until potatoes are fork-tender.

Nice to Know: A ring mold is an ideal microwave cooking dish. If you don't have a 1- or 2-quart ring mold, make one by placing an unpainted, heat-resistant drinking glass right side up in a 1 1/2-quart or 2 1/2-quart casserole.

RISOTTO

Microwave Cooking Time: 26 minutes   *4 servings*
Conventional Cooking Time: 35 minutes

1 cup long grain rice	Pinch saffron
1/4 pound mushrooms, sliced	1/2 cup dry vermouth
1 onion, chopped	1/2 cup grated Parmesan
1/4 cup butter or margarine	cheese
1 can (10 3/4 ounces) condensed chicken broth, undiluted	Salt and freshly ground pepper to taste

Microwave: Combine rice, mushrooms, onion and butter in 2-quart casserole. Cover tightly with SARAN WRAP, turning back edge to vent. Microcook at 100% power 8 minutes, stirring once. Add chicken broth and saffron. Stir, recover, leaving vent, and microcook at 100% power 3 minutes. Stir, recover and microcook at 50% power 10 minutes. Add vermouth, stir well, recover and microcook at 50% power 5 minutes longer. Let stand, covered, 5 minutes. Add Parmesan cheese and toss lightly. Season to taste with salt and pepper and serve immediately.

Conventional: Sauté rice, mushrooms and onion in hot butter until onion and rice are transparent, about 10 minutes. Reduce heat, add chicken broth, saffron, vermouth and 1/2 cup water. Stir well, cover and simmer about 25 minutes or until liquid is absorbed. Let stand 5 minutes. Add Parmesan cheese and toss lightly. Season to taste with salt and pepper and serve immediately.

SOUTHERN BEANS AND RICE

Microwave Cooking Time: 15 minutes   *6 servings*
Conventional Cooking Time: 25 minutes

1 onion, diced	Dash freshly ground
1/2 cup diced celery	pepper
2 tablespoons butter or	1 1/4 cups instant rice
margarine	2 medium-size very ripe
1 can (10 3/4 ounces)	tomatoes, chopped, or
condensed chicken	1 can (8 ounces)
broth, undiluted	stewed tomatoes
1 package (9 ounces)	1/2 cup shredded Cheddar
frozen cut green beans	cheese
3/4 teaspoon salt	

Microwave: Combine onion, celery and butter in 1 1/2-quart casserole. Cover tightly with SARAN WRAP, turning back edge to vent. Microcook at 100% power 3 minutes. Add chicken broth, beans, salt and pepper. Recover, leaving vent, and microcook at 100% power 7 minutes, stirring once. Add rice and tomatoes. Recover and microcook at 50% power 5 minutes, stirring once. Sprinkle with cheese, cover, and let stand 5 minutes before serving.

Conventional: Preheat oven to 350°. Sauté onion and celery in butter until onion is transparent, about 5 minutes. Stir in chicken broth, beans, salt, pepper, rice and tomatoes. Pour into 1 1/2-quart casserole. Bake 20 minutes. Sprinkle with cheese and let stand 5 minutes before serving.

Tempting Touches

CHEESE SAUCE

Microwave Cooking Time: 5 minutes   *1 3/4 cups*
Conventional Cooking Time: 8 minutes

2 tablespoons butter or margarine	Dash cayenne
2 tablespoons all-purpose flour	1 1/2 cups half-and-half or milk
1/2 teaspoon dry mustard	1/2 cup shredded sharp Cheddar cheese
1/4 teaspoon salt	
1/8 teaspoon freshly ground pepper	

Microwave: Place butter in 4-cup glass measure. Microcook at 100% power 1 minute. Blend in flour, mustard, salt, pepper and cayenne to make smooth paste. Add half-and-half and stir until well blended. Cover tightly with SARAN WRAP, turning back edge to vent. Microcook at 100% power 4 minutes, stirring twice with wire whisk until smooth. Stir in cheese until melted and smooth. Serve over vegetables or fish.

Conventional: Melt butter in saucepan. Blend in flour, mustard, salt, pepper and cayenne to form smooth paste. Cook 1 minute to eliminate taste of raw flour. Add half-and-half and stir until well blended. Cook over medium heat, stirring constantly, until thickened and smooth, about 5 minutes. Stir in cheese until melted and smooth. Serve over vegetables or fish.

Nice to know: Use this sauce as the base when making macaroni and cheese but increase milk and cheese to 2 cups each. Pour over 12 ounces hot cooked macaroni. Stir well, adjust seasoning and spoon into lightly greased 1 1/2-quart casserole. Cover and microcook at 70% power 12 minutes or bake, uncovered, in preheated 350° oven 30 minutes until hot and bubbly.

TEXAS BARBECUE SAUCE

Microwave Cooking Time: 10 minutes   *2 1/4 cups*
Conventional Cooking Time: 25 minutes

1 **medium-size onion, finely chopped**	3 **tablespoons cider vinegar**
1/3 **cup salad oil**	2 **tablespoons Worcester-shire sauce**
1 **can (8 ounces) tomato sauce**	2 **tablespoons chili powder**
1/2 **cup firmly packed brown sugar**	1 **teaspoon salt**

Microwave: Combine onion and oil in 4-cup glass measure. Cover tightly with SARAN WRAP, turning back edge to vent. Microcook at 100% power 2 minutes or until onion is transparent. Stir in remaining ingredients. Recover, leaving vent, and microcook at 100% power 8 minutes or until thickened, stirring once.

Conventional: Place onion and oil in small saucepan. Cook over medium heat, stirring often, until onion is transparent. Stir in remaining ingredients and heat to boiling. Reduce heat, cover and simmer 20 minutes or until thickened.

Nice to know: Use this spicy sauce on beef, pork or chicken when you cook on a grill.

FRESH TOMATO SAUCE

Microwave Cooking Time: 13 minutes   *2 1/4 cups*
Conventional Cooking Time: 35 minutes

1 **small onion, finely chopped**	1 **tablespoon red wine vinegar**
1 **clove garlic, minced**	1 **teaspoon basil**
2 **tablespoons olive oil**	1/2 **teaspoon oregano**
1 **pound fresh, very ripe tomatoes, peeled and chopped**	**Dash cloves**
	Salt and pepper to taste
1/2 **cup beef broth (use 1 cup in conventional method)**	1 1/2 **teaspoons cornstarch (optional)**
	1 **teaspoon sugar (optional)**

Microwave: Combine onion, garlic and oil in 2-quart glass bowl or casserole. Cover tightly with SARAN WRAP, turning back edge to vent. Microcook at 100% power 3 minutes. Stir in tomatoes, beef broth, vinegar, basil, oregano, cloves, salt and pepper. Blend cornstarch and sugar and stir into tomato mixture. Recover, leaving vent, and microcook at 100% power 10 minutes, stirring twice. Serve with meatloaf or pasta.

Conventional: Sauté onion and garlic in oil until onion is transparent, about 5 minutes. Stir in tomatoes, 1 cup beef broth, vinegar, basil, oregano, cloves, salt and pepper. Blend cornstarch and sugar and stir into tomato mixture. Heat to boiling. Reduce heat, cover and simmer 30 minutes or until thickened and somewhat smooth. Serve with meatloaf or pasta.

HOLLANDAISE SAUCE

Microwave Cooking Time: 2 1/2 minutes   *About 3/4 cup*
Conventional Cooking Time: 8 minutes

1/2 **cup butter**	1/8 **teaspoon salt**
3 **egg yolks**	**Dash hot pepper sauce**
2 **tablespoons lemon juice**	

Microwave: Place butter in 1-cup glass measure. Microcook at 100% power 1 minute or until melted but not hot. Combine egg yolks, lemon juice, salt and hot pepper sauce in glass bowl and stir until smooth. Stir in butter slowly. Microcook at 50% power 1 1/2 to 2 minutes, stirring every 30 seconds during first minute and every 15 seconds during second minute. (Consistency of finished sauce should be thick and smooth.) Serve over meat, fish, vegetables or eggs.

Conventional: Cut butter into 6 pieces. Beat egg yolks, lemon juice, salt and hot pepper sauce in top of double boiler. Place over (not in) barely simmering water. Add 1 piece of butter and cook, stirring constantly, until butter melts. Add next piece of butter and cook, stirring constantly, until it melts. Repeat with remaining pieces of butter. Continue cooking, stirring constantly, until sauce is slightly thickened and smooth. Serve over meat, fish, vegetables or eggs.

Nice to know: This is a very delicate sauce that may separate. If that happens, remove from heat immediately, add 1 or 2 tablespoons ice water and beat rapidly with whisk until smooth again. To keep sauce warm, set container of sauce over warm water, press SARAN WRAP directly on surface of sauce and let stand until ready to serve.

To reheat Hollandaise sauce in microwave oven, microcook at 30% power 1 1/2 to 2 minutes, stirring briskly with whisk every 30 seconds.

AVGOLEMONO SAUCE

Microwave Cooking Time: 6 1/2 minutes   *1 1/2 cups*
Conventional Cooking Time: 11 minutes

1 can (10 3/4 ounces) condensed chicken broth, undiluted	1 tablespoon chopped fresh dill or 1 teaspoon dry dill
1 scallion, sliced	1 tablespoon chopped parsley
1 teaspoon cornstarch	
2 or 3 egg yolks	Salt and freshly ground pepper to taste
2 tablespoons lemon juice	

Microwave: Combine chicken broth, scallion and cornstarch in 1 1/2-quart glass bowl or casserole. Cover tightly with SARAN WRAP, turning back edge to vent. Microcook at 100% power 4 minutes, stirring twice. Blend egg yolks and lemon juice until smooth. Gradually blend in a little hot sauce. Stir mixture back into sauce. Add dill and parsley and stir. Recover, leaving vent, and microcook at 50% power 2 1/2 minutes or until slightly thickened, stirring 3 times. Season to taste with salt and pepper. Spoon over poached, baked or broiled fish, poached eggs or steamed vegetables.

Conventional: Combine chicken broth, scallion and cornstarch in 1 1/2-quart saucepan. Heat to boiling, stirring frequently. Boil 1 minute. Blend egg yolks and lemon juice until smooth. Gradually blend in a little hot sauce. Stir egg mixture back into hot broth in saucepan. Add dill and parsley and stir. Cook over very low heat or simmering water, stirring constantly, until slightly thickened, about 8 minutes. Spoon over poached, baked or broiled fish, poached eggs or steamed vegetables.

APRICOT SAUCE

Microwave Cooking Time: 6 minutes   *1 2/3 cups*
Conventional Cooking Time: 13 minutes

1/2 cup dried apricots, diced	2 tablespoons lemon juice
1 1/4 cups pineapple juice	1/8 teaspoon cinnamon
1/2 cup sugar	1/8 teaspoon salt

Microwave: Combine apricots, pineapple juice, sugar, lemon juice, cinnamon and salt in 1 1/2-quart glass bowl or casserole. Cover tightly with SARAN WRAP, turning back edge to vent. Microcook at 100% power 6 minutes, stirring once. Let stand 5 minutes to cool slightly. Pour into blender or food processor and blend until smooth and thickened, about 1 minute. Serve warm or chilled over ice cream or cake or use to glaze pork roast, ham or chicken.

Conventional: Combine apricots, pineapple juice, sugar, lemon juice, cinnamon and salt in saucepan. Add 1/4 cup water and heat to boiling. Reduce heat, cover, and simmer 10 minutes. Let stand 5 minutes to cool slightly. Pour into blender or food processor and blend until smooth and thickened, about 1 minute. Serve warm or chilled over ice cream or cake or use to glaze pork roast, ham or chicken.

Nice to know: Make this sauce ahead of time and store in refrigerator, covered with SARAN WRAP, until ready to use.

SWEET AND SOUR RAISIN SAUCE

Microwave Cooking Time: 11 minutes   2 1/2 cups
Conventional Cooking Time: 17 minutes

1 cup port or Marsala wine	1 1/2 tablespoons cornstarch
1/2 cup raisins	1 teaspoon dry mustard
1/2 cup orange juice	1 teaspoon grated orange
1/4 cup firmly packed	peel
brown sugar	1/4 teaspoon allspice
1/4 cup red currant jelly	1/4 teaspoon salt
2 tablespoons lemon juice	Dash cloves

Microwave: Combine wine, raisins, orange juice, brown sugar, jelly, lemon juice, cornstarch, mustard, orange peel, allspice, salt and cloves in 2-quart glass bowl or casserole. Cover tightly with SARAN WRAP, turning back edge to vent. Microcook at 100% power 5 minutes, stirring twice. Stir, recover, leaving vent, and microcook at 70% power 6 minutes to blend flavors. Let stand 5 minutes. Spoon over baked ham, ham loaf, roast pork or Cornish hens.

Conventional: Combine wine, raisins, orange juice, brown sugar, jelly, lemon juice, cornstarch, mustard, orange peel, allspice, salt and cloves in saucepan. Heat to boiling, stirring constantly. Reduce heat, cover and simmer 15 minutes. Spoon over baked ham, ham loaf, roast pork or Cornish hens.

Variation: Substitute 1/4 cup chopped dried apricots for half the raisins.

RICH CHOCOLATE SAUCE

Microwave Cooking Time: 4 minutes   *1 cup*
Conventional Cooking Time: 8 minutes

3/4 cup semi-sweet
    chocolate pieces or 4
    ounces semi-sweet
    chocolate, broken
1/3 cup heavy cream or milk
    (use 1/2 cup in
    conventional method)

1/4 cup sugar
    Dash salt
2 tablespoons butter or
    margarine
1/4 teaspoon vanilla

Microwave: Combine chocolate and cream in 2-cup glass measure. Cover tightly with SARAN WRAP, turning back edge to vent. Microcook at 50% power 2 1/2 minutes, stirring once. Stir until smooth. Add sugar and salt. Recover, leaving vent, and microcook at 100% power 1 1/2 minutes or until sauce thickens, stirring once. Stir in butter and vanilla until smooth. Serve warm over ice cream.

Conventional: Combine chocolate and 1/2 cup cream in small saucepan. Cook over very low heat, stirring constantly, until chocolate melts. Stir in sugar and salt. Increase heat and cook, stirring constantly, until mixture thickens, about 5 minutes. Stir in butter and vanilla until smooth. Serve warm over ice cream.

Variation: To make Rum Chocolate Sauce, add 2 to 3 tablespoons light or dark rum to warm Rich Chocolate Sauce and stir.

Nice to know: Refrigerate leftover sauce in measuring cup tightly covered with SARAN WRAP. To reheat, microcook in covered cup at 30% power 2 to 3 minutes or until melted. Stir until smooth.

STRAWBERRY-RHUBARB MELANGE

Microwave Cooking Time: 8 minutes   *6 servings*
Conventional Cooking Time: 20 minutes

1 pound rhubarb, sliced
    (4 cups)
1/3 cup sugar
1 tablespoon cornstarch

2 teaspoons grated
    orange peel
1 quart strawberries,
    hulled and sliced

Microwave: Place rhubarb in 2-quart glass mixing bowl. Mix sugar, cornstarch and orange peel. Sprinkle over rhubarb. Toss lightly to coat. Cover tightly with SARAN WRAP, turning back edge to vent. Microcook at 100% power 6 minutes, stirring once. Add strawberries, recover, leaving vent, and microcook at 100% power 2 minutes. Serve warm or chilled.

Conventional: Place rhubarb in 3-quart saucepan. Mix sugar, cornstarch and orange peel. Sprinkle over rhubarb. Toss lightly to coat. Add 1/4 cup water and heat gently to boiling. Reduce heat, cover and simmer 15 minutes or until tender. Add strawberries and cook until just hot, about 2 minutes. Serve warm or chilled.

Nice to know: *This early summer fruit mixture is delicious over ice cream or your favorite unfrosted cake. Use it to dress up leftover cake when unexpected company appears.*

ORANGE RUM SAUCE

Microwave Cooking Time: 7 minutes   *1 1/3 cups*
Conventional Cooking Time: 15 minutes

1/4 **cup butter or margarine**	1/2 **teaspoon grated lemon**
3 **tablespoons sugar**	**peel**
1 **cup orange juice (use**	1/2 **teaspoon grated orange**
1 1/4 cups in	**peel**
conventional method)	2 **tablespoons rum**
2 **teaspoons cornstarch**	

Microwave: Combine butter and sugar in 4-cup glass measure or glass bowl. Microcook at 100% power 2 minutes. Stir in orange juice and cornstarch until smooth. Add lemon peel and orange peel. Cover tightly with SARAN WRAP, turning back edge to vent. Microcook at 100% power 5 minutes. Stir in rum. Serve over ice cream or crêpe.

Conventional: Combine butter and sugar in small saucepan. Cook and stir over low heat until sugar dissolves, about 3 minutes. Blend in orange juice and cornstarch until smooth. Add lemon peel and orange peel. Heat to boiling, stirring constantly. Reduce heat and simmer 10 minutes or until thickened and smooth. Stir in rum. Serve warm over ice cream or crêpe.

Nice to know: *To use this sauce for crêpe suzette, prepare crêpe according to your favorite recipe. Prepare sauce as above, but substitute 3 tablespoons Grand Marnier or Cointreau for rum. Pour into crêpe pan or small skillet, place over alcohol burner or low heat on range. Fold crêpe in half, then in half again and arrange in sauce. Warm gently until bubbly. Microcook 3 tablespoons brandy in glass measure at 100% power 30 seconds or heat gently on range. Pour over crêpe and ignite brandy carefully. When flame goes out, serve immediately.*

DRIED APRICOT CHUTNEY

Microwave Cooking Time: 15 minutes   *1 2/3 cups*
Conventional Cooking Time: 40 minutes

1 cup dried apricots, quartered	1/2 cup cider vinegar
2/3 cup firmly packed brown sugar	1/4 teaspoon cinnamon
	1/4 teaspoon ginger
1/2 cup chopped onion	1/4 teaspoon crushed red pepper
1/2 cup raisins	1/8 teaspoon cloves

Microwave: Combine apricots, brown sugar, onion, raisins, vinegar, cinnamon, ginger, red pepper and cloves in 2-quart glass bowl or casserole. Stir in 1/4 cup water. Cover tightly with SARAN WRAP, turning back edge to vent. Microcook at 100% power 10 minutes. Stir well. Recover, leaving vent, and microcook at 70% power 5 minutes or until thickened. Let stand 10 minutes. Store in refrigerator.

Conventional: Combine apricots, brown sugar, onion, raisins, vinegar, cinnamon, ginger, red pepper and cloves in 2-quart saucepan. Stir in 1/2 cup water and heat to boiling, stirring frequently. Reduce heat and simmer about 40 minutes or until mixture is thickened and apricots are tender. Cool and store in refrigerator.

Nice to know: Chutney is a spicy fruit condiment, delicious with meat, fish or poultry.

Dried Apricot Chutney, Pint o' Pickles (page 112),
Red and Green Pepper Relish (page 112)

PICKLED PEACHES

Microwave Cooking Time: 10 minutes   *6 servings*
Conventional Cooking Time: 17 minutes

1/2 cup cider vinegar	3 large peaches or
1/3 cup sugar	nectarines, peeled
1/4 teaspoon ginger	and quartered
1 cinnamon stick	
6 whole cloves or 1/8 teaspoon ground cloves	

Microwave: Combine vinegar, sugar, ginger, cinnamon stick and cloves in 2-quart glass bowl or casserole. Cover tightly with SARAN WRAP, turning back edge to vent. Microcook at 100% power 4 minutes or until sugar dissolves, stirring twice. Add peaches and stir to coat. Recover, leaving vent, and microcook at 100% power 6 minutes, stirring once. Let stand 30 minutes before serving. Serve warm or chilled.

Conventional: Combine vinegar, sugar, ginger, cinnamon stick and cloves in saucepan. Heat to boiling. Reduce heat, cover and simmer 5 minutes. Add peaches, cover and simmer 10 minutes or until peaches are tender. Let stand 30 minutes before serving. Serve warm or chilled.

PLUM CONSERVE

Microwave Cooking Time: 10 minutes   *2 1/2 cups*
Conventional Cooking Time: 20 minutes

1 pound plums, pitted and chopped	1/4 cup raisins
	Grated peel of 1 lemon
1 orange, seeded and finely chopped	1/2 cup chopped walnuts or pecans
1/2 cup sugar or to taste	

Microwave: Combine plums, orange, sugar, raisins and lemon peel in 3-quart glass bowl or casserole. Mix well. Cover tightly with SARAN WRAP, turning back edge to vent. Microcook at 100% power 8 minutes, stirring once. Stir in nuts, recover, leaving vent, and microcook at 100% power 2 minutes longer. Let stand, covered, 5 minutes. Stir and chill.

Conventional: Combine plums, orange, sugar, raisins and lemon peel in 3-quart saucepan. Heat to boiling, stirring constantly. Reduce heat slightly and boil gently until thickened, about 15 minutes, stirring frequently to prevent sticking. Stir in nuts and cook 2 or 3 minutes longer. Chill.

Pickled Peaches, Plum Conserve, Brandied Mushrooms (page 90)

PINT O' PICKLES

Microwave Cooking Time: 9 minutes   1 pint
Conventional Cooking Time: 18 minutes

1/2 cup cider vinegar	**Dash turmeric**
1/4 cup sugar	**2 1/2 cups sliced cucumbers**
1/2 teaspoon mustard seed	**1 small onion, thinly**
1/2 teaspoon salt	**sliced**
1/8 teaspoon celery seed	

Microwave: Combine vinegar, sugar, mustard seed, salt, celery seed and turmeric in 4-cup glass measure. Microcook at 100% power 4 minutes, stirring once. Add cucumbers and onion. Stir to coat. Cover tightly with SARAN WRAP, turning back edge to vent. Microcook at 100% power 3 minutes. Stir well and push cucumber slices into vinegar mixture. Recover, leaving vent, and microcook at 100% power 2 minutes. Let stand, covered, 10 minutes. Spoon into container, cover and chill before serving.

Conventional: Combine vinegar, 1/4 cup water, sugar, mustard seed, salt, celery seed and turmeric in small saucepan. Heat to boiling, stirring constantly. Boil 5 minutes. Add cucumbers and onion. Heat to simmering. Simmer 10 minutes or until cucumber slices are tender-crisp. Let stand, covered, 10 minutes. Spoon into container, cover and chill before serving.

RED AND GREEN PEPPER RELISH

Microwave Cooking Time: 15 minutes   2 1/4 cups
Conventional Cooking Time: 35 minutes

2 small sweet red peppers, seeded and diced	**1/2 cup vinegar**
	1/4 cup sugar
2 small sweet green peppers, seeded and diced	**1/2 teaspoon salt**
	1/4 teaspoon crushed red pepper
1 onion, chopped	**1 bay leaf**

Microwave: Combine all ingredients in 2-quart glass bowl or casserole. Stir until mixed. Cover tightly with SARAN WRAP, turning back edge to vent. Microcook at 100% power 5 minutes. Stir well, recover, leaving vent, and microcook at 70% power 10 minutes longer, stirring twice. Let stand, covered, 5 minutes. Remove bay leaf, stir and chill.

Conventional: Combine all ingredients in large saucepan. Heat gently to boiling, stirring occasionally. Reduce heat, cover and simmer 30 minutes, stirring occasionally. Remove bay leaf, stir and chill.

Nice to know: This tart-sweet relish is delicious served on hamburgers or as an accompaniment to roast meat or fish.

APPLE CHUTNEY

Microwave Cooking Time: 20 minutes   2 1/4 cups
Conventional Cooking Time: 50 minutes

1   **pound tart cooking apples, peeled and chopped**
2/3   **cup firmly packed brown sugar**
1   **medium-size onion, chopped**
1/2   **cup raisins**
1/2   **cup diced green or red pepper**

1/3   **cup cider vinegar (use 1/2 cup in conventional method)**
1/2   **teaspoon salt**
1/2   **teaspoon ginger**
1/2   **teaspoon allspice**
1/2   **teaspoon mustard seed**
1/4   **teaspoon crushed red pepper**

Microwave: Combine apples, brown sugar, onion, raisins, diced pepper, vinegar, salt, ginger, allspice, mustard seed and crushed red pepper in 3-quart glass bowl or casserole. Stir until well mixed. Cover tightly with SARAN WRAP, turning back edge to vent. Microcook at 100% power 10 minutes. Stir well. Recover, leaving vent, and microcook at 70% power 10 minutes longer, stirring once, until mixture is thickened. Let stand 10 minutes. Cool and store in refrigerator.

Conventional: Combine apples, brown sugar, onion, raisins, diced pepper, 1/2 cup vinegar, salt, ginger, allspice, mustard seed and crushed red pepper in 3-quart saucepan. Heat to boiling, stirring frequently. Reduce heat and simmer, uncovered, about 50 minutes or until mixture is thickened, stirring occasionally to prevent sticking. Cool and store in refrigerator.

Nice to know: To preserve chutneys or conserves, pour boiling hot mixture into hot half-pint canning jars, leaving 1/4-inch head space. Cover jars with new two-piece canning lids and process in water bath (not in microwave oven). Bring water to a boil and cook 10 minutes. Never process low-acid food such as meat, poultry, seafood or vegetables by this method.

RUM-RAISIN DESSERT SAUCE

Microwave Cooking Time: 8 minutes   *2 3/4 cups*
Conventional Cooking Time: 13 minutes

1/2 cup firmly packed brown sugar	1/8 teaspoon nutmeg
1/2 cup orange juice	1/8 teaspoon salt
1/4 cup lemon juice	3/4 cup raisins, coarsely chopped
2 tablespoons cornstarch	1/4 cup chopped walnuts
2 tablespoons butter or margarine	2 to 3 tablespoons rum

Microwave: Combine brown sugar, orange juice, lemon juice, cornstarch, butter, nutmeg, salt and 1 cup water in 2-quart glass bowl or casserole. Cover tightly with SARAN WRAP, turning back edge to vent. Microcook at 100% power 5 minutes, stirring twice. Stir in raisins, walnuts and rum. Recover, leaving vent, and microcook at 50% power 3 minutes. Serve warm or chilled over ice cream or cake.

Conventional: Combine brown sugar, orange juice, lemon juice, cornstarch, butter, nutmeg, salt and 1 cup water in 2-quart saucepan. Heat to boiling, stirring constantly. Boil 1 minute. Add raisins, walnuts and rum. Cover and simmer gently 10 minutes. Serve warm or chilled over ice cream or cake.

ORANGE CUSTARD SAUCE

Microwave Cooking Time: 4 minutes   *1 1/2 cups*
Conventional Cooking Time: 15 minutes

1/2 cup orange juice	2 eggs, well beaten
1/2 cup half-and-half	Dash salt
2 tablespoons sugar	

Microwave: Combine orange juice, half-and-half and sugar in 4-cup glass measure. Cover tightly with SARAN WRAP, turning back edge to vent. Microcook at 100% power 1 minute or until very warm. Beat a little of the warm juice mixture into eggs. Pour eggs back into juice mixture. Add salt, recover glass measure, leaving vent, and microcook at 50% power 3 minutes, stirring every minute until mixture thickens and is smooth. Serve warm or chilled.

Conventional: Combine orange juice, half-and-half, sugar, eggs and salt in top of double boiler. Set over (not in) simmering water and cook, stirring constantly, until sauce coats back of spoon, about 15 minutes. Serve warm or chilled.

Collector's Items

CHICKEN LIVER LUNCHEON

Microwave Cooking Time: 13 minutes   *4 servings*
Conventional Cooking Time: 16 minutes

1 medium-size onion,
    diced
1 cup sliced mushrooms
4 slices bacon, cut into
    1-inch pieces
1 pound chicken livers
1 teaspoon salt
1/8 teaspoon freshly ground
    pepper
2 tablespoons all-purpose
    flour

1/2 cup dry sherry or dry
    vermouth
1 tablespoon spicy brown
    mustard
4 servings hot cooked
    rice or 1 can (3
    ounces) chow mein
    noodles
Sliced scallions for
    garnish

Microwave: Combine onion, mushrooms and bacon in 1 1/2-quart glass bowl. Cover tightly with SARAN WRAP, turning back edge to vent. Microcook at 100% power 4 minutes. Add chicken livers, salt and pepper. Recover, leaving vent, and microcook at 70% power 5 minutes, stirring once. Stir in flour; add wine, mustard and 3/4 cup water. Stir until smooth. Recover and microcook at 100% power 4 minutes, stirring twice. Stir well and spoon over rice. Sprinkle with scallions and serve.

Conventional: Sauté onion, mushrooms and bacon in medium-size skillet until onion is transparent, about 5 minutes. Add chicken livers and sauté until lightly browned, about 5 minutes. Add flour, salt and pepper and stir. Cook 1 minute. Blend in wine, mustard and 1 1/4 cups water. Cook, stirring, until sauce is thickened and smooth. Spoon over rice. Sprinkle with scallions and serve immediately.

SPAGHETTI BROCCOLI FEAST

Microwave Cooking Time: 18 minutes　　　　　　　　*4 to 6 servings*
Conventional Cooking Time: 25 minutes

1 onion, sliced	1 teaspoon basil
2 cups sliced mushrooms	1/2 teaspoon oregano
1 clove garlic, minced	4 cups small broccoli
1/4 cup olive oil	flowerettes
3 tablespoons butter or	1/2 pound zucchini, cut
margarine	into thin strips
1/2 cup dry white wine	2 tomatoes, cut into chunks
2 tablespoons mustard,	1/2 cup half-and-half
preferably Dijon-style	1 pound spaghetti, cooked
or spicy brown	and drained
1 teaspoon salt	1 cup grated Parmesan
1/4 teaspoon pepper	cheese, divided

Microwave:　Combine onion, mushrooms, garlic, oil and butter in 4-quart casserole. Cover tightly with SARAN WRAP, turning back edge to vent. Microcook at 100% power 7 minutes, stirring once. Stir in wine, mustard, salt, pepper, basil and oregano until well mixed. Add broccoli, zucchini and tomatoes. Stir to coat. Recover, leaving vent, and microcook at 100% power 11 minutes or until broccoli is tender-crisp, stirring twice. Let stand 3 to 5 minutes. Add half-and-half and spaghetti; toss until well coated. Sprinkle with 1/2 cup Parmesan cheese and toss lightly. Serve with remaining Parmesan cheese.

Conventional:　Heat olive oil and butter in Dutch oven. Add onion, mushrooms and garlic. Sauté until onion is transparent. Add broccoli and zucchini. Cook and stir until broccoli is tender-crisp. Mix wine, mustard, salt, pepper, basil and oregano and pour over broccoli-zucchini mixture. Add tomatoes. Cover and simmer 5 minutes. Add half-and-half and spaghetti; toss until well mixed. Sprinkle with 1/2 cup Parmesan cheese and toss lightly. Serve with remaining Parmesan cheese.

Variation:　*Drain and coarsely flake 1 can (6 1/2- to 7-ounces) tuna. Add along with the spaghetti.*

BOSTON BROWN BREAD

Microwave Cooking Time: 8 minutes　　　　　　　　　*6 servings*
Conventional Cooking Time: 2 hours

1 cup whole-wheat flour	1/2 cup raisins
1/2 cup yellow cornmeal	1 cup buttermilk
1 teaspoon baking soda	1/4 cup molasses
3/4 teaspoon salt	

Microwave: Grease 1-quart casserole. Combine flour, cornmeal, baking soda and salt. Add raisins. Blend buttermilk and molasses. Stir into flour mixture. Pour batter into prepared casserole. Cover tightly with SARAN WRAP, turning back edge to vent. Microcook at 70% power 8 to 8 1/2 minutes, rotating dish twice. Cool in dish on heatproof surface 15 minutes before cutting. Cut into wedges and serve with butter.

Conventional: Grease 4-cup pudding mold or 1-pound coffee can. Combine flour, cornmeal, baking soda and salt. Add raisins. Blend buttermilk and molasses. Stir into flour mixture. Pour batter into prepared mold and cover with lid. Place mold on rack in Dutch oven. Add boiling water to come halfway up side of mold. Cover and simmer 2 hours or until cake tester inserted in center comes out clean. Remove from pan and cool in mold 10 minutes on wire rack. Invert to remove from mold and slice. Serve with butter.

CREAMED FINNAN HADDIE

Microwave Cooking Time: 13 1/2 minutes　　　　　*4 servings*
Conventional Cooking Time: 21 minutes

1 pound smoked finnan haddie or smoked cod fillets	3 tablespoons all-purpose flour
1 cup milk (use 2 cups in conventional method)	1/2 cup half-and-half or milk
1/4 teaspoon thyme	4 hard-cooked eggs, diced
1/4 teaspoon nutmeg	English muffins, halved and toasted
1 bay leaf	Chopped parsley for garnish
3 tablespoons butter or margarine	

Microwave: Cover fish with water and soak 1 hour. Drain well. Combine milk, thyme, nutmeg and bay leaf in 9 × 5-inch microsafe loaf pan or 2-quart casserole. Add fish. Cover tightly with SARAN WRAP, turning back edge to vent. Microcook at 70%

power 10 minutes, rearranging fish once. Let stand, covered, 3 minutes. Transfer fish to bowl, discard bay leaf and reserve cooking liquid. Place butter in large glass mixing bowl. Microcook at 100% power 1 1/2 minutes or until melted. Stir in flour until smooth. Add reserved liquid to flour mixture. Blend in half-and-half. Cover tightly with SARAN WRAP, turning back edge to vent. Microcook at 100% power 2 minutes, stirring twice, until thickened. Coarsely flake fish, mix with eggs and gently stir into sauce. Spoon over English muffin halves and sprinkle with parsley.

Conventional: Cover fish with water and soak 1 hour. Drain well. Combine 2 cups milk, thyme, nutmeg and bay leaf in 10-inch skillet. Heat to boiling. Add fish, cover and simmer 15 minutes. Transfer fish to bowl, discard bay leaf and reserve cooking liquid. Melt butter in saucepan. Stir in flour until smooth and cook 1 minute. Add 1 1/4 cups reserved liquid to flour mixture. Blend in half-and-half. Cook, stirring constantly, until sauce is thickened and smooth. Coarsely flake fish, mix with eggs and gently stir into sauce. Spoon over English muffin halves and sprinkle with parsley.

HOT CHICKEN SALAD

Microwave Cooking Time: 8 minutes　　　　　　　　　　*4 servings*
Conventional Cooking Time: 20 minutes

2 cups diced, cooked chicken	1 stalk celery, diced
1 can (8 ounces) water chestnuts, drained and sliced	1/2 cup mayonnaise
	1 tablespoon lemon juice
	3/4 teaspoon salt
1 can (8 ounces) pineapple chunks, drained	1/4 teaspoon ginger
	1/2 cup sliced almonds, toasted

Microwave: Combine chicken, water chestnuts, pineapple and celery in 1 1/2-quart casserole. Mix mayonnaise, lemon juice, salt and ginger. Pour over chicken and toss to coat. Cover tightly with SARAN WRAP, turning back edge to vent. Microcook at 90% power 8 minutes, stirring once. Sprinkle with toasted almonds and serve immediately.

Conventional: Preheat oven to 400°. Combine chicken, water chestnuts, pineapple and celery in 1 1/2-quart casserole. Mix mayonnaise, lemon juice, salt and ginger. Pour over chicken and toss to coat. Bake, uncovered, 20 minutes or until top is lightly browned and casserole is bubbly. Serve as above.

STEAMED CHINESE BREAD

Microwave Cooking Time: 6 1/2 minutes   *12 pieces*
Conventional Cooking Time: 42 minutes

2 tablespoons butter or margarine	3 tablespoons sugar
	1 teaspoon salt
3 cups (about) all-purpose flour, divided	1 envelope active dry yeast

Microwave: Place butter and 3/4 cup water in 1-cup glass measure. Microcook at 100% power 1/2 minute or until warm. Let stand a few minutes to melt butter. Mix 1 cup flour, sugar, salt and yeast in mixing bowl. Gradually beat in butter mixture. Beat at medium speed of electric mixer 2 minutes. Add 1/2 cup flour and beat at high speed 4 minutes. Remove from mixer and stir in 1 cup flour. Turn onto floured surface and knead until smooth and elastic, about 10 minutes, kneading in more flour as needed to keep dough from sticking. Place in greased bowl, turning to coat entire surface. Cover tightly with SARAN WRAP and place in warm (85°), draft-free place. Let rise until double in bulk, about 1 hour. Divide into 12 pieces. Shape each piece into small rectangle. Arrange dough around edge of two 9 1/2-inch unpainted wicker paper plate holders. Next, cover lightly with SARAN WRAP. Let rise until double in bulk, about 45 minutes. Pour 1 cup boiling water into 9-inch glass pie plate. Place 1 wicker plate of bread over water. Then, cover lightly with greased SARAN WRAP. Microcook at 70% power 3 minutes. Remove wicker plate from pie plate. Let stand 5 minutes before serving. Repeat with second wicker plate of bread. Cool a few minutes before serving.

Conventional: Heat butter and 3/4 cup water in small saucepan until very warm (120° to 130°). Mix 1 cup flour, sugar, salt and yeast in mixing bowl. Gradually beat in butter mixture. Beat at medium speed of electric mixer 2 minutes. Add 1/2 cup flour and beat at high speed 4 minutes. Remove from mixer and stir in 1 cup flour. Turn onto floured surface and knead until smooth and elastic, about 10 minutes, kneading in more flour as needed to keep dough from sticking. Place in greased bowl, turning to coat entire surface. Cover tightly with SARAN WRAP and place in warm (85°), draft-free place. Let rise until double in bulk, about 1 hour. Divide into 12 pieces. Shape each piece into small rectangle. Arrange dough around edge of two 9 1/2-inch unpainted wicker paper plate holders. Next, cover lightly with SARAN WRAP and let rise until double in bulk, about 45 minutes. Place wire rack in 12-inch skillet. Add 1 cup water and heat to boiling. Place 1 wicker plate of bread on rack. Cover skillet with lid and simmer 15 to 20 minutes or until bread is not doughy. (Don't lift lid to peek during first 15 minutes of steaming.) Remove wicker plate from skillet, add more water to skillet if necessary and repeat with second wicker plate of bread. Cool a few minutes before serving.

Variation: Beat 1 egg white with 1 tablespoon water. Brush over tops of raised bread. Then sprinkle lightly with toasted sesame seed, instant minced onion, garlic powder or coarse salt. Cook as directed in either method.

CRUSTLESS SPINACH QUICHE

Microwave Cooking Time: 18 minutes   *6 servings*
Conventional Cooking Time: 40 minutes

- 1/2 **cup minced onion**
- 1/4 **cup butter or margarine**
- 3 **eggs, beaten**
- 3/4 **cup half-and-half**
- 2 **packages (10 ounces each) frozen chopped spinach, thawed and squeezed dry**
- 1/2 **pound feta cheese, crumbled**
- 2 **tablespoons chopped fresh dill or 1 teaspoon dry dill**
- 1/2 **teaspoon salt**
  Dash freshly ground pepper

Microwave: Combine onion and butter in small glass bowl. Cover tightly with SARAN WRAP, turning back edge to vent. Microcook at 100% power 3 minutes. Beat eggs and half-and-half in large bowl. Stir in onion mixture, spinach, cheese, dill, salt and pepper. Pour into 10-inch microsafe quiche dish or pie plate. Cover tightly with SARAN WRAP, turning back edge to vent. Microcook at 70% power 6 minutes. Stir cooked portion to center. Recover, leaving vent, and microcook at 70% power 9 to 10 minutes longer or until almost set in center, rotating dish twice. Let stand, covered, 5 to 10 minutes until firm. Cut into wedges and serve immediately.

Conventional: Lightly butter 10-inch quiche dish or pie plate. Preheat oven to 350°. Sauté onion in butter until onion is transparent, about 5 minutes. Blend eggs and half-and-half until smooth. Stir in onion mixture, spinach, cheese, dill, salt and pepper. Pour into prepared dish. Bake 30 to 35 minutes or until knife inserted in center comes out clean. Let stand 5 minutes before serving. Cut into wedges and serve immediately.

Nice to know: To thaw spinach in microwave oven, microcook in package at 30% power 10 to 13 minutes or until soft but still cold.

BRUNCH FISH

Microwave Cooking Time: 6 minutes   *4 servings*
Conventional Cooking Time: 20 minutes

1 pound frozen flounder
  or sole fillets,
  partially thawed
4 tablespoons lemon juice,
  divided
  Salt and freshly ground
  pepper
1 large tomato, peeled
  and diced
1 small ripe avocado,
  peeled and diced

2 scallions, sliced
4 slices toast
1/4 cup mayonnaise, dairy
  sour cream or plain
  yogurt
1/2 teaspoon grated lemon
  peel
  Watercress and lemon
  wedges for garnish

Microwave: Cut partially thawed fish into 4 portions. Place in 8-inch round glass cake dish. Sprinkle with 2 tablespoons lemon juice and season with salt and pepper. Mix tomato, avocado, scallions and 1 tablespoon lemon juice. Spoon over fish. Cover tightly with SARAN WRAP, turning back edge to vent. Microcook at 100% power 6 to 8 minutes or until fish flakes easily. Let stand, covered, 5 minutes. Lift fish from baking dish with slotted spatula. Place on toast. Mix mayonnaise, lemon peel and remaining 1 tablespoon lemon juice. Spoon over fish. Garnish with watercress and lemon wedges. Serve immediately.

Conventional: Preheat oven to 350°. Cut partially thawed fish into 4 portions. Place in 8-inch baking dish. Sprinkle with 2 tablespoons lemon juice. Season with salt and pepper. Mix tomato, avocado, scallions and 1 tablespoon lemon juice. Spoon over fish. Bake 20 minutes or until fish flakes easily. Lift fish from baking dish with slotted spatula. Place on toast. Mix mayonnaise, lemon peel and remaining 1 tablespoon lemon juice. Spoon over fish. Garnish with watercress and lemon wedges. Serve immediately.

CHILIES RELLENOS RING

Microwave Cooking Time: 15 1/2 minutes   *4 servings*
Conventional Cooking Time: 40 minutes

2 cans (4 ounces each) whole green chilies, drained
1/2 pound Monterey Jack or Muenster cheese, sliced
1 2/3 cups milk
2 eggs, beaten
1/3 cup yellow cornmeal
1/2 teaspoon salt
1/2 teaspoon baking powder
Dash freshly ground pepper

Microwave: Cut chilies lengthwise in half. Remove seeds and membranes. Arrange half the chilies in 4-cup microsafe ring mold. Top with half the sliced cheese. Repeat layers of chilies and cheese. Beat milk and eggs until smooth. Blend in cornmeal, salt, baking powder and pepper. Pour over cheese and chilies in ring. Cover tightly with SARAN WRAP, turning back edge to vent. Microcook at 100% power 2 1/2 minutes. Rotate ring and microcook at 50% power 13 minutes, rotating twice. Let stand, covered, 5 minutes. Serve directly from ring mold.

Conventional: Preheat oven to 350°. Cut chilies lengthwise in half. Remove seeds and membranes. Arrange half the chilies in 4-cup ovenproof ring mold or 1-quart baking dish. Top with half the sliced cheese. Repeat layers of chilies and cheese. Beat milk and eggs until smooth. Blend in cornmeal, salt, baking powder and pepper. Pour over cheese and chilies in ring mold. Bake 35 to 40 minutes or until a knife inserted in center comes out clean. Let stand 5 minutes before serving. Serve directly from mold.

SPAETZLE

Microwave Cooking Time: 5 minutes   *4 servings as side dish*
Conventional Cooking Time: 15 minutes   *8 servings in soup*

1 1/3 cups all-purpose flour
1/2 teaspoon baking powder
Salt
2 eggs
2 to 3 tablespoons milk
2 tablespoons butter or margarine
Pepper

Microwave: Mix flour, baking powder and 1/2 teaspoon salt. Beat eggs with 2 tablespoons milk and pour into flour mixture. Stir until thick batter forms. Add additional milk if necessary. Place batter in coarse sieve or colander. Hold sieve over microsafe bowl or casserole filled with simmering, salted water. Press batter through sieve into water with back of spoon or rubber spatula. Cover tightly with SARAN WRAP, turning back edge to vent. Microcook at 70% power 5 minutes or until tender. Drain and serve in clear soup or mix with butter, salt and pepper and serve as accompaniment to main dish.

Conventional: Mix flour, baking powder and 1/2 teaspoon salt. Beat eggs with 2 tablespoons milk and pour into flour mixture. Stir until thick batter forms. Add additional milk if necessary. Place batter in coarse sieve or colander. Hold sieve over large saucepan filled with simmering, salted water. Press batter through sieve into water with back of spoon or rubber spatula. Cover and simmer gently 15 minutes or until tender. Drain and serve in clear soup or mix with butter, salt and pepper and serve as accompaniment to main dish.

Variation: Add 4 tablespoons grated Parmesan cheese, 4 tablespoons finely chopped parsley or 1 teaspoon dill to batter. It is also possible to cook spaetzle directly in soup.

EGGS IN PEPPER CUPS

Microwave Cooking Time: 7 1/2 minutes   *4 servings*
Conventional Cooking Time: 25 minutes

4 medium-size green peppers	1/4 cup milk
6 eggs, well beaten	1/2 teaspoon salt
2 scallions, sliced	1/8 teaspoon pepper
1 small tomato, finely diced	

Microwave: Slice tops off green peppers. Discard tops and remove seeds and membranes. Rinse. Place each pepper in small microsafe dish. Mix eggs, scallions, tomato, milk, salt and pepper. Pour mixture into peppers. Microcook at 70% power 7 1/2 to 8 minutes, rotating cups twice. Let stand 1 minute. Serve immediately.

Conventional: Preheat oven to 350°. Slice tops off green peppers. Discard tops and remove seeds and membranes. Rinse. Place 2 to 3 tablespoons hot water in each of 4 small ovenproof dishes. Place 1 pepper in each dish. Mix eggs, scallions, tomato, milk, salt and pepper. Pour mixture into peppers. Bake 20 to 25 minutes or until eggs are set and puffy.

BRAN MUFFINS

3/4 **cup wheat bran cereal**	1 1/2 **teaspoons baking powder**
1/2 **cup milk (use 2/3 cup in conventional method)**	1/4 **teaspoon salt**
1/2 **cup all-purpose flour**	1 **egg**
1/4 **cup firmly packed brown sugar**	3 **tablespoons vegetable oil**

Microwave: Line 8 custard cups or microsafe muffin pans with paper liners. Combine cereal and milk. Let stand 5 minutes. Mix flour, brown sugar, baking powder and salt. Combine egg and oil and add to cereal mixture. Beat until well combined. Add flour mixture to cereal mixture and stir until well mixed. Spoon into paper-lined muffin cups, filling each cup only half full. Arrange cups in circle in microwave oven. Microcook at 70% power 4 1/2 to 5 minutes rotating cups after half cooking time. Let stand on heatproof surface 5 minutes

Conventional: Preheat oven to 400°. Line 8 muffin cups with paper liners. Combine ingredients as directed in microwave method, but increase milk to 2/3 cup. Spoon into 8 paper-lined muffin cups, filling each cup only half full. Bake 20 to 25 minutes or until muffins are golden brown.

Nice to know: Cover muffins with SARAN WRAP to keep them fresh. To reheat one muffin in a microwave oven, wrap in SARAN WRAP and microcook at 50% power 20 seconds.

CHICKEN-STUFFED ARTICHOKES

Microwave Cooking Time: 17 minutes   *4 servings*
Conventional Cooking Time: 45 minutes

4 medium-size artichokes	1/4 teaspoon salt
Salt	1/4 teaspoon tarragon or
1 cup cooked, minced	dill
chicken	Dash freshly ground
1/4 cup minced celery	pepper
2 tablespoons minced	Avgolemono Sauce
onion	(page 104), Hollandaise
1 tablespoon lemon juice	Sauce (page 103) or
2 tablespoons mayonnaise	mayonnaise
or dairy sour cream	

Microwave: Cut artichoke stems flat with bottom of artichokes. Trim off thorny tip of each leaf with scissors. Place artichokes, stem ends down, in 1 1/2-quart casserole. Add 1/3 cup lightly salted water and cover tightly with SARAN WRAP, turning back edge to vent. Microcook at 100% power 10 minutes. Turn artichokes, stem end up, recover, leaving vent, and microcook at 100% power 3 minutes longer or until artichokes are almost tender. Let stand, covered, 10 minutes. Uncover and allow to cool until easy to handle. Pull artichoke leaves out from center, exposing small thorn-tipped leaves inside. Remove small center leaves and scrape out fuzzy "choke" in bottom with spoon. Rinse and drain. Mix chicken, celery, onion, lemon juice, mayonnaise, 1/4 teaspoon salt, tarragon and pepper. Spoon into centers of artichokes. Place filled artichokes upright in 1 1/2-quart casserole. Cover tightly with SARAN WRAP, turning back edge to vent. Microcook at 90% power 4 minutes or until filling is hot. Serve immediately with warm sauce or mayonnaise.

Conventional: Prepare artichokes as directed in microwave method. Place in lightly salted boiling water. Cover and simmer 20 to 25 minutes or until artichokes are almost tender. Cool until easy to handle. Pull artichoke leaves out from center, exposing small thorn-tipped leaves inside. Remove small center leaves and scrape out fuzzy "choke" in bottom with spoon. Rinse and drain. Preheat oven to 350°. Mix chicken, celery, onion, lemon juice, mayonnaise, 1/4 teaspoon salt, tarragon and pepper. Spoon into centers of artichokes. Place filled artichokes upright in casserole. Bake 15 to 20 minutes or until filling is hot. Serve immediately with warm sauce or mayonnaise.

Sweet Conclusions

BANANA SNACK CAKE

Microwave Cooking Time: 7 minutes   *4 to 6 servings*
Conventional Cooking Time: 25 minutes

1 cup whole wheat flour	1/3 cup vegetable oil
1/2 cup firmly packed brown sugar	1 egg, beaten
1 teaspoon baking powder	Confectioners sugar (optional)
1/4 teaspoon baking soda	
1/4 teaspoon salt	
1/2 cup mashed, very ripe banana (2 small bananas)	

Microwave: Lightly grease 4-cup microsafe ring mold. Mix flour, brown sugar, baking powder, baking soda and salt in large bowl. Combine banana, oil and egg and stir until blended. Add to flour mixture and stir until smooth. Pour into prepared ring mold. Cover tightly with SARAN WRAP, turning back edge to vent. Microcook at 50% power 6 minutes, rotating dish once. Rotate dish again and microcook at 100% power 1 to 1 1/2 minutes or until top of cake is almost dry. Cool, covered, 10 minutes on heatproof surface. Cover with plate and invert to remove from mold. Serve warm or cold. Dust with confectioners sugar if desired.

Conventional: Lightly grease 4-cup ovenproof ring mold or baking dish. Preheat oven to 350°. Prepare batter as directed in microwave method. Pour into prepared dish and bake 25 minutes or until toothpick inserted in center comes out clean. Cool on rack. Cover with plate and invert to remove from mold. Serve warm or cold. Dust with confectioners sugar if desired.

Nice to know: To keep this moist, delicate cake fresh, cover cooled cake tightly with SARAN WRAP and store at room temperature.

JAM CAKE

Microwave Cooking Time: 6 minutes   *6 servings*
Conventional Cooking Time: 25 minutes

1 cup all-purpose flour	1 egg
1 teaspoon cinnamon	1/4 cup buttermilk (use 1/2
3/4 teaspoon baking soda	cup in conventional
1/4 teaspoon salt	method)
1/2 cup sugar	1/2 cup red raspberry jam
1/3 cup vegetable oil	

Microwave: Grease 8-inch round glass baking dish. In large bowl, mix flour, cinnamon, baking soda and salt. Combine sugar, oil and egg. Add flour mixture and buttermilk and stir until smooth. Pour batter into prepared baking dish. Cover tightly with SARAN WRAP, turning back edge to vent. Microcook at 50% power 5 minutes, rotating dish twice. Rotate again and microcook at 100% power 1 to 1 1/2 minutes or until top of cake is barely moist when touched. Let stand on heatproof surface, covered, 15 minutes. Remove from pan, spread with raspberry jam and serve warm.

Conventional: Grease 8-inch round baking dish. Preheat oven to 350°. Prepare cake batter as directed in microwave method, but increase buttermilk to 1/2 cup. Bake 20 to 25 minutes or until cake tester inserted in center comes out clean. Cool in pan on wire rack 15 minutes. Remove from pan, spread with raspberry jam and serve warm.

CARROT CAKE

Microwave Cooking Time: 8 1/2 minutes   *6 servings*
Conventional Cooking Time: 35 minutes

1 cup all-purpose flour	1/3 cup vegetable oil
1 teaspoon baking soda	1/4 cup buttermilk (use 1/2
1/2 teaspoon salt	cup in conventional
1 teaspoon cinnamon	method)
1/4 teaspoon nutmeg	1 cup shredded carrots
1/4 teaspoon cloves	1/4 cup chopped nuts
1 cup firmly packed	Pineapple Cream Cheese
brown sugar	Frosting (page 131)
1 egg	

Microwave: Lightly grease 8-inch round glass baking dish. Combine flour, baking soda, salt, cinnamon, nutmeg and cloves. Beat sugar, egg, oil and buttermilk until smooth and stir in carrots. Add carrot mixture and nuts to flour mixture. Stir just until moistened. Pour batter into prepared baking dish. Cover tightly with SARAN WRAP, turning back edge to vent. Microcook at 70% power 8 1/2 to 9 minutes or until surface of cake is fairly dry. (There will be a moist, partially cooked spot in center of cake.) Cool, covered with SARAN WRAP, on heatproof surface. Remove cake from pan and spread with Pineapple Cream Cheese Frosting.

Conventional: Grease 8-inch round or square baking dish. Preheat oven to 350°. Prepare cake batter as directed in microwave method but increase buttermilk to 1/2 cup. Pour batter into prepared pan. Bake 30 to 35 minutes or until center springs back when lightly pressed. Cool on wire rack. Remove cake from pan and spread with Pineapple Cream Cheese Frosting.

PINEAPPLE CREAM CHEESE FROSTING

1 package (3 ounces) cream cheese, softened	Dash salt
1/4 cup crushed pineapple	1 3/4 to 2 cups confectioners sugar

Beat cream cheese, pineapple and salt, until well mixed. Add confectioners sugar, beating until frosting is spreading consistency. Add additional sugar if necessary. Spread over cooled Carrot Cake.

CRANBERRY WINE WARMER

Microwave Cooking Time: 15 minutes   *6 servings*
Conventional Cooking Time: 25 minutes

3 cups cranberry juice cocktail	2 sticks cinnamon
2 oranges, sliced	1/4 teaspoon cardamom
1 lemon, sliced	3 cups dry red wine

Microwave: Combine cranberry juice, orange slices, lemon slices, cinnamon sticks and cardamom in heatproof pitcher or 2-quart glass bowl. Cover tightly with SARAN WRAP, turning back edge to vent. Microcook at 100% power 10 minutes. Stir in wine, recover, leaving vent, and microcook at 100% power 5 minutes or until steaming hot. Serve in mugs.

Conventional: Combine cranberry juice, orange slices, lemon slices, cinnamon sticks and cardamom in saucepan. Heat gently to simmering. Cover and simmer 15 minutes. Add wine and heat to just piping hot, about 5 minutes. Serve in mugs.

CHOCOLATE CAKE

Microwave Cooking Time: 14 minutes   *2 8-inch layers*
Conventional Cooking Time: 35 minutes

1/2 cup shortening	1 1/2 teaspoons baking soda
1 1/4 cups sugar	3/4 teaspoon salt
3 eggs	3/4 cup milk (use 1 1/4 cups
2 ounces (2 squares)	in conventional method)
unsweetened chocolate,	1 teaspoon vanilla
melted	Chocolate Cream
1 3/4 cups all-purpose flour	Frosting (page 134)

Microwave: Grease two 8-inch round glass cake dishes. Beat shortening and sugar together until light and fluffy. Add eggs one at a time, beating well after each addition. Beat in chocolate. Mix flour, baking soda and salt. Add flour mixture alternately with milk to chocolate mixture, beating well after each addition. Stir in vanilla. Pour batter into prepared baking dishes. Microcook one layer at a time at 50% power 5 1/2 minutes, rotating once. Rotate layer again and microcook at 100% power 1 1/2 to 2 minutes or until center of layer is nearly dry. (The surface may appear slightly moist, but when touched gently, the crust layer will come off and reveal a dry, cooked cake.) Place cake dish on heatproof surface. Cover tightly with SARAN WRAP and allow to cool 10 minutes. Remove cake by inverting pan and cool completely. Repeat with second layer. Fill and frost with Chocolate Cream Frosting or wrap in SARAN WRAP to preserve freshness for future use. Fill and frost just before serving.

Conventional: Grease two 8-inch round cake pans. Preheat oven to 350°. Prepare cake batter as directed in microwave method, but increase milk to 1 1/4 cups. Pour batter into prepared pans. Bake 35 minutes or until cake tester inserted in center comes out clean. Cool in pans on wire rack 10 minutes. Invert pans to remove cake layers, and cool completely on wire racks. Fill and frost with Chocolate Cream Frosting or wrap in SARAN WRAP to preserve freshness for future use. Fill and frost just before serving.

Poached Pears (page 134) with Rich Chocolate Sauce (page 106),
Chocolate Cake with Chocolate Cream Frosting (page 134)

CHOCOLATE CREAM FROSTING

1/2 cup butter or margarine,
    softened
3 squares (3 ounces)
    unsweetened chocolate,
    melted
1 package (16 ounces)
    confectioners sugar

3 to 4 tablespoons milk
    or half-and-half
1/2 teaspoon vanilla
2 egg yolks

Beat butter and chocolate in small mixer bowl until smooth and creamy. Gradually add sugar alternately with milk. Beat in vanilla and egg yolks. If necessary, add additional milk to improve spreading consistency.

Nice to know: To melt chocolate in microwave oven, place unwrapped squares in small glass bowl. Microcook at 50% power 3 to 3 1/2 minutes. Let stand 2 to 3 minutes. Stir until smooth.

POACHED PEARS

Microwave Cooking Time: 12 minutes   *6 servings*
Conventional Cooking Time: 20 minutes

6 ripe pears
2/3 cup dry white wine (use
    1 cup in conventional
    method)
3/4 cup sugar

2 tablespoons lemon juice
1 cinnamon stick
1/4 teaspoon almond extract
    Rich Chocolate Sauce
    (page 106)

Microwave: Peel pears but do not remove stems. Cut out blossoms with tip of knife. Set aside. Combine wine, sugar, lemon juice, cinnamon stick and almond extract in 2-quart round casserole. Cover tightly with SARAN WRAP, turning back edge to vent. Microcook at 100% power 2 minutes. Arrange pears in circle in casserole with stem ends toward center of dish. Recover, leaving vent, and microcook at 70% power 10 to 12 minutes or until pears are fork-tender. Turn pears over once during cooking. Chill pears in wine mixture. To serve, spoon pears into dessert dishes and top with spoonful of Rich Chocolate Sauce.

Conventional: Peel pears but do not remove stems. Cut out blossoms with tip of knife. Set aside. Combine 1 cup wine, sugar, lemon juice, cinnamon stick and almond extract in 10-inch skillet. Heat to boiling. Reduce heat, cover and simmer 5 minutes. Add pears, turning to coat with wine mixture. Simmer 15 to 20 minutes or until fork-tender. Chill pears in wine mixture. To serve, spoon pears into dessert dishes and top with spoonful of Rich Chocolate Sauce.

PINEAPPLE-ORANGE CHIFFON PIE

Microwave Cooking Time: 6 minutes　　　　　　*6 to 8 servings*
Conventional Cooking Time: 15 minutes

2/3 cup sugar, divided	1 cup heavy cream
2 envelopes unflavored gelatin	1 9-inch baked Pie Shell (page 141) or Graham Cracker Crumb Crust (page 156)
1/4 teaspoon salt	Orange sections
1 cup orange juice	Mint sprigs
1 tablespoon grated orange peel	
3 eggs, separated	
1 can (8 ounces) crushed pineapple	

Microwave: Combine 1/3 cup sugar, gelatin and salt in 1 1/2-quart glass bowl or casserole. Add orange juice and orange peel and stir until well mixed. Cover tightly with SARAN WRAP, turning back edge to vent. Microcook at 100% power 3 minutes, stirring once. Lightly beat egg yolks. Beat a little hot orange juice mixture into yolks. Stir yolk mixture back into hot sauce. Recover, leaving vent, and microcook at 50% power 3 minutes, or until slightly thickened, stirring twice. Stir in undrained pineapple. Place a piece of SARAN WRAP directly on surface of orange mixture and refrigerate until cooled and thickened, about 1 hour 15 minutes.

Beat egg whites until soft peaks form. Sprinkle in remaining 1/3 cup sugar and continue beating until stiff and glossy. Set aside. Beat cream until soft peaks form. Stir large spoonful of beaten whites into pineapple-orange mixture. Fold in remaining egg whites. Fold in whipped cream. Spoon into pie shell and chill until set, about 2 hours. Garnish with orange sections and mint sprigs.

Conventional: Combine 1/3 cup sugar, gelatin and salt in saucepan. Add orange juice and orange peel. Cook and stir over medium heat until gelatin dissolves, about 5 minutes. Lightly beat egg yolks. Beat a little hot orange juice mixture into yolks. Stir yolk mixture back into hot sauce. Cook over very low heat, stirring constantly, until slightly thickened, about 10 minutes. Stir in undrained pineapple. Pour into medium-size bowl. Place a piece of SARAN WRAP directly on surface of orange mixture. Refrigerate until cooled and thickened, about 1 hour 15 minutes. Beat egg whites and cream and combine ingredients as directed in microwave method. Garnish with orange sections and mint sprigs.

APPLE SPICE CAKE

Microwave Cooking Time: 15 minutes   *8 servings*
Conventional Cooking Time: 35 minutes

1 cup whole wheat flour	2 cups coarsely chopped
1/4 cup crushed bran cereal	apples
1 teaspoon baking soda	1/2 cup chopped nuts
1/2 teaspoon cinnamon	1 egg
1/2 teaspoon salt	1/3 cup cooking oil
1 cup firmly packed brown sugar	

Microwave: Grease 8-inch square glass baking dish. Combine flour, cereal, baking soda, cinnamon and salt. Add sugar, apples and nuts. Beat egg and oil until well combined. Pour over apple-flour mixture and stir until mixture is evenly moistened. Pour into prepared baking dish. Microcook at 70% power 15 minutes, rotating dish 1/4 turn every 5 minutes. Cover with SARAN WRAP and let stand on heatproof surface until completely cooled. Cut into bars and serve with ice cream or sprinkled with confectioners sugar.

Conventional: Grease 8-inch square baking dish. Preheat oven to 350°. Combine flour, cereal, baking soda, cinnamon and salt. Add sugar, apples and nuts. Beat egg and oil until well combined. Pour over apple-flour mixture and stir until mixture is evenly moistened. Pour into prepared baking dish. Bake 35 minutes or until center springs back when lightly pressed. Cool completely in pan on wire rack. Serve as above.

Nice to know: Cover leftover cake snugly with SARAN WRAP to keep cake moist and fresh.

HOT BUTTERED RUM

Microwave Cooking Time: 7 minutes   *4 servings*
Conventional Cooking Time: 7 minutes

1/4 cup firmly packed brown sugar	2 tablespoons butter or margarine
4 cinnamon sticks	3/4 cup rum
4 lemon twists	
Nutmeg	

Microwave: In each of 4 microsafe mugs, place 3/4 cup water, 1 tablespoon sugar, 1 cinnamon stick, a lemon twist and a sprinkling of nutmeg. Cover tightly with SARAN WRAP, turning back edge to vent. Microcook at 100% power 7 minutes or until water boils. Add 1/2 tablespoon butter to each mug and stir to melt. Stir 3 tablespoons (1 jigger) rum into each mug and serve immediately.

Conventional: Heat 3 cups water to boiling. Place 1 table-spoon brown sugar, 1 cinnamon stick, a lemon twist and 1/2 tablespoon butter in each of four mugs or heatproof glasses. Pour 3/4 cup boiling water into each mug. Let stand 2 to 3 minutes to allow flavors to develop. Stir 3 tablespoons (1 jigger) rum into each mug, sprinkle with nutmeg and serve immediately.

Nice to know: *You can use either light or dark rum for this drink. Dark rum will provide a richer, sweeter flavor than light rum.*

LEMON SHORTBREAD

Microwave Cooking Time: 9 minutes   *6 to 8 servings*
Conventional Cooking Time: 30 minutes

1/2 cup butter or margarine, softened	3/4 cup confectioners sugar
1/4 cup sugar	2 teaspoons grated lemon peel
Dash salt	1/4 cup lemon juice
1 1/4 cups all-purpose flour	1/4 teaspoon baking powder
3 eggs	

Microwave: Beat butter, sugar and salt until smooth. Add flour and mix until well blended. Press into bottom of 8-inch round glass cake dish. Microcook at 100% power 4 minutes, rotating dish once. Beat eggs until light and frothy. Beat in confectioners sugar, lemon peel, lemon juice and baking powder. Pour over shortbread crust. Cover tightly with SARAN WRAP, turning back edge to vent. Microcook at 70% power 5 minutes or until custard is set about 1 inch from center. Cool, covered, on heatproof surface. To serve, sprinkle with additional confectioners sugar and cut into wedges.

Conventional: Preheat oven to 350°. Beat butter, sugar and salt until smooth. Add flour and mix until well blended. Press into bottom of 8-inch round cake dish. Bake 15 to 20 minutes or until firm, but not brown. Beat eggs well. Blend in confectioners sugar, lemon peel, lemon juice and baking powder until smooth. Pour over shortbread crust. Bake 15 to 18 minutes or until set. Cool in pan on wire rack. To serve, sprinkle with additional confectioners sugar and cut into wedges.

Nice to know: *To soften butter, microcook at 30% power 20 seconds. Let stand about 1 minute. If butter is wrapped in foil, remove wrapper and place on plate.*

RAISIN BARS

Microwave Cooking Time: 17 minutes *12 bars*
Conventional Cooking Time: 30 minutes

1 cup dark seedless raisins, chopped	1/2 cup firmly packed brown sugar
1/2 cup orange juice	1 teaspoon vanilla
2 tablespoons granulated sugar	1 teaspoon baking powder
3/4 cup chopped walnuts, divided	1 1/2 cups quick cooking oats
1/2 cup butter or margarine, softened	3/4 cup all-purpose flour

Microwave: Mix raisins, orange juice and granulated sugar in medium-size glass bowl. Cover tightly with SARAN WRAP, turning back edge to vent. Microcook at 70% power 5 minutes or until thickened, stirring 2 or 3 times. Stir in 1/4 cup nuts. Set aside. Cream butter, brown sugar and vanilla until fluffy. Beat in baking powder. Add oats, flour and remaining 1/2 cup nuts. Reserve 1 1/2 cups oat mixture. Press remaining oat mixture into 8-inch square glass baking dish. Microcook at 50% power 6 minutes or until there are no wet spots on surface, rotating dish once. Spread reserved raisin mixture over base. Cover with reserved 1 1/2 cups oat mixture. Microcook at 100% power 6 minutes or until top looks dry, rotating 1/4 turn every two minutes. Cool on heatproof surface. Cut into 12 bars.

Conventional: Grease 8-inch square baking dish. Preheat oven to 350°. Combine raisins, orange juice and granulated sugar in small saucepan. Cook over medium heat, stirring constantly until thickened, about 5 minutes. Stir in 1/4 cup nuts. Set aside. Combine remaining ingredients as directed in microwave method and reserve 1 1/2 cups oat mixture. Press remaining oat mixture into prepared dish. Spread with reserved raisin mixture and cover with reserved oat mixture. Bake 25 to 30 minutes. Cool in pan on wire rack. Cut into 12 bars.

Nice to know: To keep raisins from sticking to knife, toss with 1 teaspoon vegetable oil and chop on wooden board. In a food processor or blender, add 1 teaspoon vegetable oil to 1 cup raisins and process about 1 minute. If a recipe calls for a dry ingredient like flour or bread crumbs, add to raisins instead of oil before chopping in food processor.

Raisin Bars, Lemonade Concentrate (page 140),
Streusel Apple Pie (page 140)

STREUSEL APPLE PIE

Microwave Cooking Time: 15 minutes   *6 to 8 servings*
Conventional Cooking Time: 45 minutes

3/4 cup firmly packed brown sugar	2 pounds tart cooking apples, peeled and sliced (6 to 7 cups)
3 tablespoons cornstarch	
2 tablespoons lemon juice	One 9-inch baked Pie Shell (page 141) (use unbaked Pie Shell in conventional method)
1 teaspoon cinnamon	
1/2 teaspoon nutmeg	
1/8 teaspoon cloves	
Dash salt	

Streusel Topping:

3 tablespoons butter or margarine, melted	1/2 teaspoon cinnamon
1/2 cup all-purpose flour	1/2 teaspoon baking powder
3 tablespoons sugar	1/8 teaspoon salt

Microwave: Combine brown sugar, cornstarch, lemon juice, cinnamon, nutmeg, cloves and salt in large bowl. Add sliced apples and toss until well coated. Distribute evenly in baked pie shell; set aside. For topping, place butter in glass bowl. Microcook at 100% power 1 minute or until melted. Stir in flour, sugar, cinnamon, baking powder and salt. Drop by teaspoonfuls evenly over apples. Microcook at 100% power 14 minutes, rotating pie once. Cool on wire rack.

Conventional: Preheat oven to 400°. Make pie filling and topping as directed in microwave method, using unbaked pie shell. Bake 40 to 45 minutes or until apples are tender and topping is lightly browned. Cool on wire rack.

LEMONADE CONCENTRATE

Microwave Cooking Time: 4 minutes   *6 servings*
Conventional Cooking Time: 5 minutes

3/4 cup sugar	3/4 cup lemon juice
2 tablespoons grated lemon peel	Mint leaves for garnish

Microwave: Combine sugar, lemon peel and 3/4 cup water in 4-cup glass measure. Cover tightly with SARAN WRAP, turning back edge to vent. Microcook at 100% power 4 to 5 minutes or until sugar dissolves. Stir in lemon juice. Cover with

SARAN WRAP and refrigerate. To serve, pour 1/3 cup lemon concentrate over ice, add 1 cup water and stir. Garnish with mint leaves.

Conventional: Combine sugar, lemon peel and 3/4 cup water in small saucepan. Heat to boiling. Reduce heat, cover and simmer 3 minutes. Stir in lemon juice. Cover with SARAN WRAP and refrigerate. To serve, pour 1/3 cup lemon concentrate over ice, add 1 cup water and stir. Garnish with mint leaves.

Variation: To make limeade, substitute lime peel and lime juice for lemon peel and lemon juice.

Nice to know: Grate citrus peel before squeezing out juice. Use a fine grater and grate the colored portion only, leaving the tart, white pith on the fruit.

PIE SHELL

Microwave Cooking Time: 4 1/2 minutes   *1 9-inch pie shell*
Conventional Cooking Time: 12 minutes

1 cup all-purpose flour
1/2 teaspoon salt
1/3 cup shortening
About 3 tablespoons ice water

3 drops yellow food coloring (optional — use in microwave method only)

Microwave: Mix flour and salt. Cut in shortening with pastry cutter or 2 knives until mixture resembles coarse crumbs. Mix ice water with food coloring if desired. Add water, 1 tablespoon at a time, tossing with fork after each addition, until pastry is moistened and holds together. Gather pastry into ball and roll 1/8-inch thick on lightly floured surface. Fit loosely into 9-inch glass pie plate. Trim overhang to 1/2 inch. Fold overhang under and pinch to make decorative edge. Prick pastry at 1/2-inch intervals with fork. Microcook at 100% power 4 1/2 to 5 minutes or until pastry is opaque. Cool completely before filling.

Conventional: Preheat oven to 425°. Prepare pastry and line pie plate as above. (Do not add food coloring.) Prick well. Bake 12 to 15 minutes or until golden brown. Cool completely on wire rack.

Nice to know: Pat pastry into flat circle, wrap in SARAN WRAP and store in refrigerator or freezer if desired. Bring almost to room temperature before rolling.

STRAWBERRY RHUBARB SOUFFLE

Microwave Cooking Time: 9 minutes .... *6 to 8 servings*
Conventional Cooking Time: 20 minutes

4 cups sliced rhubarb	1 pint strawberries
1 cup sugar, divided	3 egg whites
1 envelope unflavored gelatin	1 cup heavy cream

Microwave: Make 2-inch wax paper collar on 4-cup glass soufflé dish. Combine rhubarb and 3/4 cup sugar in 2-quart casserole. Cover tightly with SARAN WRAP, turning back edge to vent. Microcook at 100% power 8 to 10 minutes until mixture boils and rhubarb is tender, stirring once. Refrigerate, covered, until well chilled. Sprinkle gelatin over 1/4 cup water in small bowl. Let stand 3 minutes. Microcook at 100% power 1 minute or until hot. Stir until gelatin dissolves. Cool to room temperature.

Reserve one or more strawberries for garnish. Clean and coarsely chop remaining berries. Set aside. Beat egg whites until soft peaks form. Sprinkle in 1/4 cup sugar and continue beating until stiff. Reduce speed and gradually beat in gelatin mixture. Set aside. Beat cream until soft peaks form. Set aside. Combine chopped strawberries and 1 cup chilled rhubarb mixture in bowl. Fold in beaten egg whites. Fold in half of whipped cream. Pour remaining rhubarb mixture into prepared soufflé dish. Top with strawberry-rhubarb mixture. Smooth top and chill until set, about 4 hours. Dollop remaining half of whipped cream on top of soufflé and garnish with whole strawberries. To serve, spoon fluffy portion of soufflé onto dessert plates and top with rhubarb sauce from bottom of dish.

Conventional: Prepare soufflé dish as directed in micro-wave method. Combine rhubarb, 3/4 cup sugar and 1/4 cup water in large saucepan. Cook over medium heat until rhubarb is tender, approximately 15 minutes. Place in bowl, cover with SARAN WRAP and refrigerate until well chilled. Sprinkle gelatin over 1/4 cup water in small saucepan. Let stand 3 minutes. Cook and stir over low heat 4 to 5 minutes until gelatin dissolves. Cool to room temperature. Clean strawberries and assemble soufflé as directed in microwave method. Chill well and serve as above.

MOCHA-ORANGE WARMER

Microwave Cooking Time: 6 minutes   *4 servings*
Conventional Cooking Time: 6 minutes

1/3 cup sugar	2 tablespoons cocoa
1/4 cup frozen orange juice	Whipped cream
concentrate, thawed	2 orange slices, cut
3 tablespoons instant	in half
coffee powder	

Microwave: Combine sugar, orange juice concentrate, instant coffee, cocoa and 2 1/2 cups water in 4-cup glass measure. Cover tightly with SARAN WRAP, turning back edge to vent. Microcook at 100% power 6 minutes or until steaming hot. Stir until smooth. Pour into 4 heatproof mugs and top with whipped cream. Cut slit in halved orange slices and hook on mugs. Serve immediately.

Conventional: Combine sugar, orange juice concentrate, instant coffee, cocoa and 2 1/2 cups water in saucepan. Heat until steaming hot, stirring often, about 6 minutes. Pour into 4 heatproof mugs and top with whipped cream. Cut slit in halved orange slices and hook on mugs. Serve immediately.

ORANGE GINGERBREAD

Microwave Cooking Time: 10 minutes   *8 servings*
Conventional Cooking Time: 28 minutes

1/4 cup molasses	1 teaspoon baking soda
1/4 cup orange juice	3/4 teaspoon ginger
1/4 cup butter or margarine	1/4 teaspoon cinnamon
1 cup all-purpose flour	1/4 teaspoon cloves
1/2 cup firmly packed brown	1/4 teaspoon salt
sugar	Orange Custard Sauce
1 tablespoon grated	(page 114), whipped cream
orange peel	or ice cream

Microwave: Grease 8-inch round glass baking dish. Combine molasses, orange juice and butter in 2-cup glass measure. Cover tightly with SARAN WRAP, turning back edge to vent. Microcook at 100% power 2 1/2 minutes or until very hot. Let stand. Meanwhile combine flour, brown sugar, orange peel, baking soda, spices and salt in mixing bowl. Add molasses mixture and stir until well blended. Pour batter into prepared baking dish. Cover tightly with SARAN WRAP, turning back edge to vent. Microcook at 50% power 5 minutes, rotating dish once.

Microcook at 100% power 2 1/2 to 3 minutes or until top of cake is almost dry. Cool on heatproof surface at least 10 minutes. Serve warm with Orange Custard Sauce, whipped cream or ice cream.

Conventional: Grease 8-inch round or square baking dish. Preheat oven to 350°. Combine molasses, orange juice and butter in small saucepan. Heat until butter melts and mixture is simmering. Mix flour, brown sugar, orange peel, baking soda, spices and salt in mixing bowl. Add molasses mixture and stir until well blended. Pour into prepared baking dish. Bake 25 minutes or until toothpick inserted in center comes out clean. Cool slightly in dish on wire rack. Serve warm with Orange Custard Sauce, whipped cream or ice cream.

BAKED CUSTARD

Microwave Cooking Time: 14 minutes   *6 servings*
Conventional Cooking Time: 1 hour, 20 minutes

2 1/2 cups milk (use 3 cups in conventional method) 4 eggs	1/2 cup sugar 1/8 teaspoon salt 1 teaspoon vanilla Nutmeg

Microwave: Place milk in 4-cup glass measure. Cover tightly with SARAN WRAP, turning back edge to vent. Microcook at 100% power 4 to 5 minutes or until steaming hot. Beat eggs, sugar and salt. Gradually beat in hot milk. Stir in vanilla. Pour into 4-cup microsafe ring mold. Microcook at 50% power 7 minutes, stirring twice. Stir well and sprinkle with nutmeg. Microcook at 50% power 3 to 5 minutes longer or until custard is nearly set. Rotate ring mold every minute. Remove from oven and cover with SARAN WRAP. Cool on heatproof surface 30 minutes. Chill well. Serve with fresh fruit or toasted coconut.

Conventional: Lightly butter 1-quart casserole or heatproof ring mold. Preheat oven to 300°. Heat 3 cups milk in saucepan over low heat until tiny bubbles form around edge. Stir often to prevent skin from forming on top of milk. Beat eggs, sugar and salt. Gradually beat in hot milk. Pour into prepared dish. Sprinkle with nutmeg. Place in larger baking dish and add boiling water to come halfway up side of dish. Bake 1 hour 15 minutes or until knife inserted in custard comes out clean. Remove custard from water bath and cool on wire rack. Chill well. Serve with fresh fruit or toasted coconut.

CHOCOLATE POTS DE CREME

Microwave Cooking Time: 5 1/2 minutes   *6 to 8 servings*
Conventional Cooking Time: 15 minutes

2 cups heavy cream, divided	2 teaspoons grated orange peel
1 package (6 ounces) semi-sweet chocolate pieces	1 teaspoon orange-flavored liqueur
1/4 cup granulated sugar Dash salt	1 teaspoon confectioners sugar
4 egg yolks	

Microwave: Combine 1 1/2 cups cream, chocolate pieces, granulated sugar and salt in 4-cup glass measure. Cover tightly with SARAN WRAP, turning back edge to vent. Microcook at 100% power 4 minutes or until mixture is steaming and chocolate melts, stirring twice. Beat egg yolks in small mixer bowl at medium speed. Beat in cream mixture until just blended. Return mixture to 4-cup measure, recover, leaving vent, and microcook at 50% power 1 1/2 minutes, stirring twice. Stir in orange peel. Pour into small dessert dishes or demi-tasse cups. Chill well. To serve, whip remaining 1/2 cup cream, add orange-flavored liqueur and confectioners sugar. Spoon over servings of dessert.

Conventional: Heat 1 1/2 cups cream, chocolate, granulated sugar and salt over very low heat, stirring constantly until melted, about 10 minutes. Beat egg yolks in small mixer bowl at medium speed. Beat in chocolate mixture until just blended. Return chocolate-egg mixture to saucepan. Cook, stirring constantly, until mixture thickens slightly. Stir in orange peel. Pour into small dessert dishes or demi-tasse cups. Chill well. To serve, whip remaining 1/2 cup cream, add orange-flavored liqueur and confectioners sugar. Spoon over desserts.

Variation: Make Mocha Pots de Crème by using only 1/2 package (3 ounces) semi-sweet chocolate pieces. Add 1 tablespoon instant coffee powder to cream before melting chocolate.

Nice to know: Since this is a very rich dessert, small portions are appropriate.

PLUM COMPOTE

Microwave Cooking Time: 13 minutes   *5 servings*
Conventional Cooking Time: 25 minutes

1 1/2 cups sugar	1 stick cinnamon
1 cup dry red wine	1 1/2 pounds red or purple
Grated peel of 1 orange	plums (about 10)
Grated peel of 1 lemon	1/4 cup toasted slivered
1 teaspoon anise seed	almonds

Microwave: Combine sugar, wine, orange peel, lemon peel, anise seed and cinnamon in 2-quart glass casserole. Cover tightly with SARAN WRAP, turning back edge to vent. Microcook at 100% power 5 minutes or until sugar dissolves, stirring once. Add plums, after picking with toothpick or thin skewer to prevent skin from bursting. Recover, leaving vent, and microcook at 100% power 8 to 10 minutes or until plums are fork-tender, stirring plums once. If desired, strain cooking liquid. Serve warm or well chilled, sprinkled with almonds.

Conventional: Combine sugar, wine, orange peel, lemon peel, anise seed and cinnamon in large saucepan. Bring to a boil. Simmer 5 minutes. Add plums, cover and simmer 15 to 20 minutes or until plums are fork-tender. If desired, strain cooking liquid. Serve warm or well chilled, sprinkled with almonds.

CURRIED FRUIT

Microwave Cooking Time: 12 minutes   *8 servings*
Conventional Cooking Time: 33 minutes

1 cup dry white wine	4 peaches, cut into chunks
or dry vermouth	4 plums, cut into chunks
1/2 cup firmly packed brown	1 cup seedless green
sugar	grapes
1 tablespoon cornstarch	1/4 cup sliced almonds,
2 or 3 teaspoons curry	toasted
1/2 teaspoon salt	Lime wedges for garnish
3 medium-size bananas,	
cut into chunks	

Microwave: Mix wine, brown sugar, cornstarch, curry and salt in 4-cup glass measure. Cover tightly with SARAN WRAP, turning back edge to vent. Microcook at 100% power 4 minutes, stirring twice. Place fruit in 2 1/2-quart glass bowl. Pour sauce over fruit; stir gently to coat. Cover tightly with SARAN WRAP, turning back edge to vent. Microcook at 90% power 8 minutes, stirring once. Sprinkle with almonds and garnish with lime wedges. Serve warm or chilled.

Conventional: Preheat oven to 350°. Combine wine, brown sugar, cornstarch, curry and salt in saucepan. Heat to boiling, stirring constantly. Boil 1 minute. Combine fruit in 2 1/2-quart casserole. Pour sauce over fruit; stir gently to coat. Bake 30 minutes. Sprinkle with almonds and garnish with lime wedges. Serve warm or chilled.

Nice to know: Use fruit that is barely ripe and still firm. Ripe fruit is likely to get mushy. Serve as an accompaniment to ham or chicken or over rice.

RICE PUDDING

Microwave Cooking Time: 40 minutes   *6 servings*
Conventional Cooking Time: 1 hour, 30 minutes

4 **cups milk**	1/4 **teaspoon cinnamon**
2/3 **cup long grain rice**	1/4 **teaspoon salt**
1/2 **cup sugar**	2 **eggs, beaten**
1/2 **cup dark seedless**	**Strawberry preserves**
raisins	
1 **tablespoon grated**	
orange peel	

Microwave: Combine milk and rice in 2-quart casserole. Cover tightly with SARAN WRAP, turning back edge to vent. Microcook at 100% power 7 minutes, stirring once. Stir in sugar, raisins, orange peel, cinnamon and salt. Recover, leaving vent, and microcook at 50% power 30 minutes, stirring twice. Beat a little hot rice mixture into eggs. Pour egg mixture into casserole and blend. Microcook at 50% power 3 minutes or until set, rotating casserole once. Serve warm with strawberry preserves.

Conventional: Grease 2-quart casserole. Preheat oven to 325°. In saucepan, heat rice and 3/4 cup water to boiling. Reduce heat, cover and simmer 10 minutes. Gradually add milk and sugar. Heat until tiny bubbles form around edge of saucepan. Stir in raisins, orange peel, cinnamon and salt. Place beaten eggs in casserole and gradually beat in hot milk mixture. Place casserole in large baking dish and add boiling water to come halfway up side of casserole. Bake 1 hour 15 minutes or until knife inserted in center comes out clean. Serve warm with strawberry preserves.

CHERRIES JUBILEE

Microwave Cooking Time: 9 minutes   *6 to 8 servings*
Conventional Cooking Time: 18 minutes

2/3 cup sugar	1 1/2 pounds sweet or bing
2 tablespoons cornstarch	cherries, pitted
1/8 teaspoon salt	1/3 cup cognac
1/2 cup sweet red wine	1 quart vanilla ice cream

Microwave: Combine sugar, cornstarch and salt in 3-quart glass bowl or casserole. Stir in 1/2 cup water and wine until smooth. Add cherries and cover tightly with SARAN WRAP, turning back edge to vent. Microcook at 100% power 8 to 9 minutes or until cherries are tender and sauce is thickened, stirring once. Meanwhile, scoop ice cream into dessert dishes. Place cognac in 1-cup glass measure. Microcook at 100% power 30 to 40 seconds or until warm. Pour cherries into shallow serving dish. Pour warmed cognac gently and evenly over cherries. Ignite carefully with long match. When flame goes out, ladle cherries over ice cream and serve immediately.

Conventional: Combine sugar, cornstarch and salt in 3-quart saucepan. Stir in 3/4 cup water and wine until smooth. Add cherries and heat to boiling. Reduce heat, cover and simmer 12 to 15 minutes or until cherries are tender and sauce is thickened, stirring occasionally. Meanwhile, scoop ice cream into dessert dishes. Pour cognac into small saucepan and place over low heat until just warm. Pour cherries into shallow serving dish. Pour warmed cognac gently and evenly over cherries. Ignite carefully with long match. When flame goes out, ladle cherries over ice cream and serve immediately.

APPLE-RUM WARMER

Microwave Cooking Time: 11 minutes   *4 servings*
Conventional Cooking Time: 15 minutes

3 2/3 cups apple juice
  1/4 cup firmly packed
        brown sugar
  1/4 cup lemon juice
    1 stick cinnamon, broken

1 teaspoon whole cloves
1 tablespoon whole allspice
1/2 cup dark rum
4 lemon slices

Microwave: Combine apple juice, brown sugar, lemon juice, cinnamon stick, cloves and allspice in 4-cup glass measure. Cover tightly with SARAN WRAP, turning back edge to vent. Microcook at 100% power 6 minutes. Stir, recover, leaving vent, and microcook at 50% power 5 minutes longer. Strain into 4 heatproof mugs, add 2 tablespoons rum to each mug and top with lemon slices.

Conventional: Combine apple juice, brown sugar, lemon juice, cinnamon stick, cloves and allspice in medium-size saucepan. Heat slowly to boiling. Reduce heat, cover and simmer gently 12 minutes. Strain into 4 mugs, add 2 tablespoons rum to each mug and top with lemon slices.

Nice to know: Apple cider is a good substitute for apple juice. Serve with Orange Gingerbread (page 144) or Apple Spice Cake (page 136).

ZABAGLIONE

Microwave Cooking Time: 2 3/4 minutes   *4 to 6 servings*
Conventional Cooking Time: 12 minutes

  4 egg yolks
  1 whole egg
1/4 cup super-fine sugar

Dash salt
1/2 cup sweet or dry
      marsala wine or sherry

Microwave: Place egg yolks, egg, sugar and salt in 2 1/2-quart glass mixing bowl. Beat at high speed of electric mixer 5 minutes or until thick and fluffy. Place marsala in 1-cup glass measure. Microcook at 100% power 45 seconds or until warm. Reduce mixer speed to medium and gradually beat warm marsala into egg-yolk mixture. Microcook at 50% power 2 to 2 1/2 minutes, stirring every 30 seconds or until mixture is double in volume, slightly thickened and warm. Serve immediately with cookies or over chilled fresh fruit.

Conventional: Place egg yolks, egg, sugar and salt in top of double boiler. Beat at high speed of electric mixer 5 minutes or until thick and fluffy. Reduce speed to medium and gradually beat in unwarmed marsala. Place over (not in) simmering water and cook, beating constantly, until mixture is double in volume, slightly thickened and mounds when beater is lifted. Serve immediately with cookies or over chilled fresh fruit.

PINA COLADA PIE

Microwave Cooking Time: 5 1/2 minutes   *6 to 8 servings*
Conventional Cooking Time: 20 minutes

1 envelope unflavored gelatin	1/4 cup dark rum
2/3 cup canned pineapple juice	1 cup heavy cream
3 eggs, separated	9-inch Baked Pie Shell (page 141), cooled
3/4 cup sugar, divided	Mint leaves and sliced pineapple for garnish

Microwave: Sprinkle gelatin over pineapple juice in 2-quart glass bowl. Let stand 3 minutes. Microcook at 100% power 1 1/2 minutes or until hot. Stir until gelatin dissolves. Beat egg yolks and 1/2 cup sugar. Blend into pineapple juice mixture until smooth. Microcook at 50% power 4 minutes, stirring every minute, until thickened. Stir in rum. Press SARAN WRAP directly onto surface of pineapple mixture and chill until thickened, stirring occasionally, about 40 minutes.

Beat egg whites until soft peaks form. Sprinkle in 1/4 cup sugar and continue beating until stiff and glossy. Set aside. Beat cream until soft peaks form. Stir large spoonful of beaten whites into pineapple mixture. Fold in remaining egg whites. Fold in whipped cream. Spoon into pie shell and chill until set. Garnish with mint leaves and pineapple.

Conventional: Sprinkle gelatin over pineapple juice in 1-quart saucepan. Let stand 3 minutes. Cook and stir over low heat 4 or 5 minutes until gelatin dissolves. Beat egg yolks and 1/2 cup sugar. Blend into pineapple juice mixture until smooth. Cook over very low heat, stirring constantly, until thickened, 10 to 15 minutes. Stir in rum. Pour mixture into medium-size bowl. Press SARAN WRAP directly onto surface of pineapple mixture and chill until thickened, stirring occasionally, about 40 minutes. Beat egg whites and cream and combine ingredients as directed in microwave method. Spoon into pie shell and chill until set. Garnish with mint leaves and pineapple.

STEAMED PUMPKIN PUDDING

Microwave Cooking Time: 17 minutes   *8 servings*
Conventional Cooking Time: 1 hour, 18 minutes

3 tablespoons butter or margarine	1/4 teaspoon ground cloves
1 cup raisins	1 1/2 teaspoons baking soda
1 1/4 cups all-purpose flour	1/2 teaspoon salt
1 cup firmly packed brown sugar	1 cup canned pumpkin
1 teaspoon cinnamon	2 eggs, well beaten
1/2 teaspoon nutmeg	Whipped cream or ice cream

Microwave: Grease 2-quart microsafe ring mold. Combine butter, raisins and 2 tablespoons water in medium-size glass mixing bowl. Cover tightly with SARAN WRAP, turning back edge to vent. Microcook at 100% power 2 minutes or until butter melts and raisins are puffed. Mix flour, brown sugar, cinnamon, nutmeg, cloves, baking soda and salt. Stir into raisin mixture. Add pumpkin and eggs and stir until smooth. Pour batter into prepared mold. Cover tightly with SARAN WRAP, turning back edge to vent. Microcook at 50% power 13 minutes, rotating twice. Rotate and microcook at 100% power 2 minutes or until toothpick inserted in center comes out almost clean. Cool, covered, on heatproof surface 10 minutes. Cover with serving plate and invert to remove pudding from mold. Serve warm with whipped cream or ice cream.

Conventional: Grease 6- to 7-cup mold. Combine butter, raisins and 2 tablespoons water in small saucepan. Cook over low heat, stirring occasionally, until butter melts. Combine dry ingredients; add raisin mixture; stir in pumpkin and eggs until smooth. Pour batter into prepared mold. Cover with lid. Place on rack in large, deep saucepan of simmering water. If necessary, add boiling water to come about halfway up sides of mold. Cover saucepan and simmer 1 hour 15 minutes or until cake tester inserted in center comes out clean. Let stand 5 minutes. Cover with serving plate and invert to remove pudding from mold. Serve warm with whipped cream or ice cream.

CHEESECAKE

Microwave Cooking Time: 13 1/2 minutes   *8 servings*
Conventional Cooking Time: 55 minutes

Crust

- 3 tablespoons butter or margarine
- 3 tablespoons sugar
- 1 cup chocolate cookie or vanilla wafer crumbs

Filling

- 2 packages (8 ounces each) cream cheese, softened
- 3 eggs
- 1/3 cup sugar
- 1 cup dairy sour cream, divided
- 2 teaspoons grated lemon peel
- 1 teaspoon vanilla
- 1/8 teaspoon salt
- 2 tablespoons confectioners sugar
- Halved strawberries for garnish

Microwave: Place butter in 8-inch round glass cake dish. Microcook at 100% power 1 minute. Stir in sugar and crumbs. Mix well and press crust into bottom of dish. Microcook at 100% power 2 1/2 minutes, rotating once. Set aside to cool. Beat cream cheese in glass mixing bowl until smooth. Beat in eggs, one at a time. Beat in sugar, 1/4 cup sour cream, lemon peel, vanilla and salt. Cover tightly with SARAN WRAP, turning back edge to vent. Microcook at 100% power 4 to 5 minutes or until mixture begins to thicken, stirring every minute. Pour into crust. Microcook at 50% power 5 minutes or until set, rotating twice. Mix remaining 3/4 cup sour cream and confectioners sugar. Spread over top of cake. Microcook at 50% power 1 minute. Cool on heatproof surface. Chill before serving. Arrange strawberry halves on cake just before serving.

Conventional: Preheat oven to 350°. Melt butter and stir in sugar and crumbs. Press crust into bottom of 9-inch springform pan. Bake 8 to 10 minutes or until lightly browned. Cool. Decrease oven temperature to 325°. Beat cream cheese until smooth. Beat in eggs, one at a time. Beat in sugar, 1/2 cup sour cream, lemon peel, vanilla and salt. Pour into cooled crust. Bake 40 minutes or until set. Mix remaining 1/2 cup sour cream with confectioners sugar. Spread over top of cake and bake 5 minutes longer or until sour cream is set. Cool completely on wire rack. Carefully loosen side of cake from pan. Chill before serving. Arrange strawberry halves on cake just before serving.

GRAHAM CRACKER CRUMB CRUST

Microwave Cooking Time: 3 1/2 minutes　　　　　*1 pie shell*
Conventional Cooking Time: 10 minutes

1/4 cup butter or margarine	**1/4 cup sugar**
1 1/3 cups graham cracker crumbs	**1/4 teaspoon salt**

Microwave:　Place butter in 9-inch glass pie plate. Microcook at 100% power 1 1/2 minutes until melted. Stir in crumbs, sugar and salt until evenly moistened. Press onto bottom and sides of pie plate, using custard cup or back of spoon. Microcook at 100% power 2 minutes, rotating once. Cool completely on wire rack before filling. Cover tightly with SARAN WRAP and store in refrigerator until ready to fill.

Conventional:　Preheat oven to 375°. Melt butter in small saucepan over low heat. Stir in crumbs, sugar and salt until evenly moistened. Press onto bottom and sides of pie plate, using custard cup or back of spoon. Bake 8 to 10 minutes or until lightly browned. Cool completely on wire rack before filling. Cover tightly with SARAN WRAP and store in refrigerator until ready to fill.

Variations:　Substitute vanilla, chocolate or gingersnap cookie crumbs for graham cracker crumbs, but use only 1 or 2 tablespoons sugar, or omit sugar entirely. To make a Nut Crumb Crust, substitute 1/2 cup ground nuts for 1/2 cup cookie crumbs.

Nice to know:　Use a food processor to make cookie crumbs and to grind nuts. If your crumbs are not evenly ground, sift them before adding them to remaining ingredients. Large pieces of cracker cause the crust to break when the pie is served.

Index